In Step With the Master

A. Okechukwu Ogbonnaya, Ph.D.
AUTHOR

LEADER'S GUIDE
written by
Denise K. Gates

Urban Ministries, Inc.
Chicago, Illinois

Publisher
Urban Ministries, Inc.
P. O. Box 436987
Chicago, IL 60643-6987
1.800.860.8642

First Edition
First Printing
ISBN: 0-940955-54-7

Copyright ©1999 by Urban Ministries, Inc. All rights reserved. No part of this publication may be reproduced, stored in a retrieval system, or transmitted in any form or by any means, electronic, mechanical, photocopy, recording, or otherwise except for brief quotations in printed reviews without prior written permission from the holder of the copyright.

Scripture quotations are taken from the King James Version of the Bible unless otherwise stated. Printed in the United States of America.

TABLE OF CONTENTS

SESSION 1
You Are Called by the Master   9

SESSION 2
By the Word You are Equipped   20

SESSION 3
You Are Invited   31

SESSION 4
You Are Made Whole   44

SESSION 5
You Have the Authority   55

SESSION 6
Jesus Will Come For You   66

SESSION 7
On Being Loyal
to Jesus as Lord   79

SESSION 8
You Can Believe   93

SESSION 9
You Can Depend
on God's Promises   105

SESSION 10
You Are Chosen   117

PREFACE

This Leader's Guide is designed for use with the devotional book In Step With the Master.

Jesus is calling each of us to deny ourselves, take up our cross and follow Him. Many of us have answered His call. We have willingly responded, "Yes Lord, I will follow you." But we are unsure about exactly how to do so. What would Jesus have us to do? How do we follow Jesus? *In Step With the Master* is designed to help churches and individuals answer these questions by presenting a basic, step-by-step approach to Christian living.

The purpose of this Leader's Guide is to direct and assist leaders who wish to use In Step With the Master for group Bible study. Each Bible study participant should have a copy of the book, In Step With the Master and the Student Workbook. Both the Leader's Guide and Student Workbook are organized in 10 Bible study sessions which correspond to the 10 chapters of the devotional book.

For each session, the Leader's Guide contains:

Lesson Format and Directions for Group Study—directions for a two-part Bible Study lesson which can be tailored to fit the size and duration of the individual group.

Lesson Aims and Prayer Focus.

Scripture Search—questions, activities, and points for discussion of the Scripture passage.

Chapter Highlights—selected definitions and an outline of chapter topics to facilitate review and discussion in a group setting.

Bible Study Questions and Answers—six to eight multiple part questions which allow participants to examine the Word of God and explore the biblical truths for themselves.

Personal Application Questions—three to five questions which encourage participants to evaluate their personal walk with God and challenge them to apply the Word of God in their own lives.

Church Ministry Application Questions—three questions which encourage participants to incorporate biblical truth in their corporate lives as members of the local body of believers and in the ministries of their local church.

In summary, the Leader's Guide contains recommended structure, background information, related activities, and answers to the Bible Study Application questions for each session of Bible study. Due to the nature of the Life Application questions, answers for the Personal Application and Church Ministry Application questions are not provided.

Uses. This book can be used in a variety of ways. Although this Leader's Guide is designed to facilitate group study, it can be used for both private study and family devotions, as well. Group study of the material can be conducted in private, home-study groups or within the local church setting. In the church, the Leader's Guide can be used to train teachers and deacons, and for Sunday School electives, Training Hour curriculum, adult Vacation Bible School curriculum, as well as weekday Bible studies on Christian living.

Group Study—90-Minute Sessions. A 90-minute group session is divided into two-parts. In Part One, participants discuss the Scripture and the corresponding chapter of the book. During Part Two, the session leader divides the group into smaller groups to answer and discuss the Bible Study Application questions. The small group discussions provide each participant with an opportunity to contribute to the group's understanding and application of the material. In the final discussion, the participants reconvene with the larger group and report their findings and review the Life Application questions.

Group Study—60-Minute Sessions. For shorter periods, only Part One of the lesson format would be used. Participants discuss the Scripture, the assigned chapter of *In Step With the Master,* and the related background information during the group meeting. If time permits, selected Bible Study Application questions can be used as a stimulus for discussion. The remaining Bible Study Application and Life Application questions might be used as a "homework" assignment or for private devotional study.

Church-Wide Retreats and Leadership Training. When all or part of a weekend is available, a study of *In Step With the Master* can be conducted in a number of ways. For example, 10 people could be assigned to lead a workshop on a different chapter. Participants would read the entire book prior to the retreat or scheduled training. Then, they would be encouraged to select a chapter to study in depth, and then enroll in the workshop devoted to that chapter.

In the opening session, the overall leader (pastor, minister, special speaker, or lay leader) would give a presentation on the theme: "What It Means to Follow Christ Today" to set the tone and focus of the study. This presentation could be general (exploring historical and contemporary issues related to African American Christian living), or specific (challenging participants to examine and apply the information to the local church body).

After the opening session, participants would attend the workshops that focus on a particular chapter. These sessions should include general discussion, personal application, and produce specific suggestions and/or strategies for church ministry.

The final session would be devoted to small group discussion and reports. These reports should be given by representatives from each workshop. This final discussion would also involve sharing the answers to the Church Ministry Application section of each chapter. These suggestions may be used to plan activities for the upcoming church calendar year.

Family Devotions. Before the study of a particular chapter, each member would read the chapter privately and do the Bible Study Application questions. In devotions, the family would first discuss the chapter. Then each member could present his or her answers, opinions, and insights "round robin style." The devotion should end with personal application and prayer.

Preparing Participants for the Discussion. To prepare for the Bible study, participants should read the assigned chapter of *In Step With the Master* before each session. Encourage participants to take time to think through the material as they read and study. Ask them to come prepared to share thoughts, Scriptures, or experiences related to information presented in the chapter. Thus, participants can contribute to the discussion—improving the depth and detail of the ideas exchanged.

Leading the Discussion. Several techniques can be used to lead group discussions. Effective leadership always requires good preparation. Begin by reading *In Step With the Master* from beginning to end. Take notes, underline interesting or important passages, and jot down ideas which come to you.

Then survey the entire Leader's Guide. Knowing which topics will be covered, and when, will help you conduct each session more effectively. If questions come up concerning topics that will be covered in a later session, you may choose to postpone the discussion until that time. Also, feel free to tailor or modify the session to meet the needs of your group.

Before each Bible Study session:
1. Pray for wisdom.
2. Know the goal.
3. Depend on the Holy Spirit.
4. Review the material.
5. Gather any supplies or additional information you may needed.

During each session:
1. Begin with prayer.
2. Maintain a relaxed, informal atmosphere.
3. Keep track of the time.
4. Keep the discussion moving by asking probing questions, restating the topic, and pointing out the differences between the world's view and God's view.
5. Focus on biblical truths.
6. Encourage participants to evaluate their lifestyles, goals, and objectives and to apply the biblical truths to their own lives so that they can walk *In Step With the Master* in the world today.

SESSION ONE

YOU ARE CALLED BY THE MASTER

For sessions of 90 minutes or more, use the lesson format for PART ONE and PART TWO.

PART ONE

ACTIVITY	TIME
Opening Prayer	5 minutes
Scripture Search	10 minutes
Chapter Highlights	20 minutes

PART TWO

ACTIVITY	TIME
Small Group Study	15 minutes
Large Group Presentations	25 minutes
Large Group Discussion	10 minutes
Closing Prayer	5 minutes

For sessions of less than 90 minutes, use PART ONE only and assign the Bible Study Application questions as homework.

Lesson Aims: At the end of this two-part Bible study session, the participants should be able to: a) examine Jesus' call to the disciples and their response; b) realize that Jesus is calling each of us to follow Him; c) consider their personal response to the call of the Master; d) understand what it means to be a follower of Jesus; e) make or reaffirm their own commitment to follow Christ.

PART ONE

A. OPENING PRAYER

Open the session with prayer. Include the requests that God would bless each participant to:

- Understand the urgency and importance of their spiritual calling.
- Consider the costs as well as the benefits of following the Master.
- Become a true follower of Jesus Christ.

B. SCRIPTURE SEARCH

1. Ask someone to read

Matthew 4:18-22 and 9:9 aloud to the group.

2. Ask for volunteers to answer the following questions:
   - Describe the response of Simon Peter and his brother Andrew to the call of Jesus.
   "And they straightway left their nets, and followed him" (Matthew 4:20).

   - Describe the response of James and John to the call of Jesus.
   "And they immediately left the ship and their father, and followed him" (v. 22).

   - Describe the response of Matthew to the call of Jesus.
   "And he arose, and followed him" (Matthew 9:9b).

3. In light of the disciples' examples and the truths from Chapter One, invite the participants to seriously consider their own response to the call of the Master.

C. CHAPTER HIGHLIGHTS

Before discussing the chapter, define the following terms:

Spiritual Calling—A divine command or request to come; a sacred summons; an authoritative instruction or direction; a divine invitation.

A Follower—One who: goes after, seeks, or goes in pursuit of someone or something; moves behind in the same direction; or believes in and adheres to the authority of another as a leader. (Note: to become followers we must take action.)

Following Christ—To respond to the divine invitation to seek Christ; to become Christ's believers, disciples (students), imitators, and servants who obey His Word and perform His will on earth.

Bible Background: The Example of Jesus

1. Point out that Jesus, as the Son of Man, had a very special call on His life. Ask the class "What was Jesus called to do?"
   Answers will vary; be sure that the following truths are mentioned:
   - Jesus came to take away our sin (John 1:29).
   - Jesus came to bring the light of truth (John 8:12).
   - Jesus came to repair the relationship between God

and man (John 14:6).
- Jesus came to give us eternal life (John 3:15-16).
- Jesus came to provide abundant life (John 10:10)

2. Ask someone to read the account of Jesus' temptation in the wilderness from Matthew 4:1-11 aloud to the group. Discuss the following:
    - Satan's goal in tempting Jesus.
    - How Jesus responded to temptation.
    - What we can learn from His example.

3. Point out that Jesus chose to follow the call of God, even at the expense of some human relationships.
    - Ask someone to summarize the relationship between Jesus and John the Baptist.
    - Ask the class: "How do you think Jesus felt when He heard that John had been cast into prison?"
    - Point out that by beginning His earthly ministry the same way that John began, by preaching "Repent: for the kingdom of heaven is near" (Matthew 4:17), Jesus both honors John's ministry and demonstrates His own humility in following the plan of God (see also John 6:38).

Chapter Discussion

Using the content of Chapter One as background, give a general overview of the chapter. Be sure to include the following topics:
1. Whose Call Do We Follow?
2. How Can We Hear (and Distinguish) the Master's Voice?
3. What Is Required of True Followers of Christ?
4. What Is the Purpose of Jesus' Call?
5. Why Must We Respond Immediately?
6. What Are the Benefits of Following Christ?

PART TWO

A. BIBLE STUDY APPLICATION
1. Introduction

The Bible Study Application section contains five questions which provide an opportunity to examine what the Bible says about following Christ and to consider how we can apply these principles to our lives today. The discussion of the Bible Study Application questions should confirm that the students understand the basic definitions and concepts of discipleship.

Allow as much time as necessary to encourage free participation and exchange of ideas and insights. Use the information preceding each set of questions to help introduce or close the discussion of a topic. Use the Bible verses to help keep the discussion on track. Depending on the size and personality of the group, you can discuss as many or as few of the questions as needed.

2. Procedure

Select Small Group Leaders. Ask for volunteers or select five small group leaders. Then assign each small group leader a number from 1-5. (This can also be done beforehand to save time.) Ask the small group leaders to write their numbers on large sheets of white paper so that they can be seen from a distance.

Divide into Small Groups. Inform the participants that they will be separated into small groups. Each group will study a different set of questions and then will present their findings to the larger group at the end of the study period. The questions should be assigned as follows:

Group #1: Hearing the Master's Call (question 1)
Group #2: Responding to the Master's Call (question 2)
Group #3: Walking in Step with the Master (question 3)
Group #4: The Cost of Following the Master (question 4)
Group #5: The Benefits of Following the Master (question 5)

Allow Participants to Count Off by Fives. Then ask them to follow the small group leader who is holding their assigned number. Identify the location of each group. (These locations can also be pre-printed on a sheet of paper, photocopied, and distributed to save time.) Participants should then assemble into smaller groups in their respective meeting areas.

Note: If the Bible Study is small, divide into four groups and eliminate discussion group #5. You may want to include question 5 as part of the homework assignment.

B. SMALL GROUP STUDY

1. Small Group Leaders

Each group will have one topic to explore. For each topic, there is a multi-part question and related Scripture references to stimulate discussion.

   2. **Sharing Insights**
   After 15 minutes, designate someone who will summarize the small group discussion within the larger body of participants. Remind the designated person that she or he will only have five minutes to present.

C. LARGE GROUP PRESENTATIONS
   Reconvene the Group. Call the small groups back together.

   Explain the Procedure. Explain that a representative of each small group will share that group's reflections on the Bible Study Application questions with the larger group.

   Remind Small Group Representatives of the Time. Remind each group representative that he or she should try to summarize the group's discussion in less than five minutes. Allow up to five minutes to discuss each group's presentation.

D. LIFE APPLICATION DISCUSSION*
   If time permits, the larger group can then discuss the Personal Application and Church Ministry questions together.

   1. **Introduction**
   The Personal Application section contains five questions which encourage the participants to consider the teaching in light of their own lives. The Church Ministry Application section contains three questions which address some implications for the congregation as a whole.

   2. **Sharing Insights**
   This discussion should be open-ended and voluntary. The sharing of personal insights or recommendations for church ministry should be encouraged but not required. The group may have quite a bit to say. Watch the clock! Stop them after 10 minutes.

   *Answers are not provided for the Personal Application and Church Ministry sections because of the personal or specific nature of the questions.

E. PREPARATION FOR NEXT MEETING
   Assignment. Have the participants read Chapter Two, "By the Word You Are Equipped" and review the questions in preparation for next week's

session. Encourage them to come to the next session prepared to share their insights on the content of the chapter.

You may also want to assign small groups or particular questions to facilitate next week's meeting time.

F. CLOSING PRAYER

Hold hands, form a circle, and ask for specific prayer requests. Then ask for several volunteers to pray, keeping the prayer requests in mind.

ANSWERS TO BIBLE STUDY APPLICATION

Hearing the Master's Call
Jesus said, "My sheep hear my voice, and I know them, and they follow me" (John 10:27).

1. Look up the verses below to determine how we can "hear" the voice of the Master today.
   a) Romans 10:17 and 1 Thessalonians 2:13
      We hear the voice of the Master through God's Word, the Bible.
      Our faith comes by hearing and believing the Word of God.
   b) John 20:31; Hebrews 1:1-2 and 1 John 5:11-12
      We hear the voice of the Master through the testimony of Jesus Christ. God's call was issued first through the prophets and is now given to us through His Son.
   c) John 14:26; 16:13-14 and 1 Corinthians 2:9-10
      We hear the voice of the Master by following the leadership and the promptings of the Holy Spirit.
   d) Mark 16:15 and Romans 10:14-15
      We hear the voice of the Master by listening to the pastors and teachers who preach the Word of God and bring the Good News of the Gospel of Jesus Christ.

Responding to the Master's Call
The very first step in following the Master is to answer the call of salvation. This calling supercedes our gender, culture, class, and occupation. It

is a call to "come home" spiritually—to be united with the Father as members of the body of Christ and the family of God.

2. Using the verses below, review the answers to these basic questions regarding salvation. Discuss any new insights you receive.
    a) Who is God calling to be saved? (John 3:16-17; Romans 10:13; 1 Timothy 2:3-4)
    God's divine offer of salvation goes out to everyone. God is calling each of us to receive salvation through faith in Jesus Christ. Whosoever will hear and answer God's call will be saved.
    b) How can we hear the call of salvation? (Acts 2:37; Hebrews 3:15; 1 John 5:13)
    We hear God's call of salvation when we truly consider and decide to believe the Word of God and the Gospel of Jesus Christ.
    c) How do we answer the call of salvation? (Acts 3:19; 16:30-31; Romans 10:9-10)
    From the beginning of His ministry, Jesus' message was a call to: "Repent and believe" (Mark 1:15; cf. Matthew 4:17). To repent is to turn from our self-centered, sinful life and to turn to Him. We answer the call of salvation by: 1) Admitting that we are sinners and repenting; 2) Believing (having faith) that Jesus was the Son of God, that His death on the cross was divine payment for our sins, and that His resurrection is proof of His deity and our redemption; 3) Confessing and making Jesus Christ the Lord of our life; and 4) Committing ourselves to follow Him.
    d) How do we obtain salvation? (Ephesians 2:8-9; Titus 2:11; 3:5)
        By the mercy and grace of God we are saved. We obtain righteousness and the gift of eternal life through faith in Christ Jesus our Saviour.

Walking in Step with the Master
To walk with the Master, we must move. We must go from where we are to where He is. We must allow Him to determine our direction, our goals, and our purpose in life.

3. Match the following Scripture references with the ways that we should follow the Master.

   a. Hebrews 11:6 and 2 Peter 1:10   e. Immediately
   b. Matthew 6:33 and Romans 8:28   b. Purposefully
   c. Jeremiah 29:13 and Mark 12:30   g. Faithfully
   d. John 15:14 and James 1:22   c. Wholeheartedly
   e. Isaiah 55:6 and Revelation 22:17   f. Daily
   f. Luke 9:23 and Hebrews 3:13-14   d. Obediently
   g. Hebrews 6:12 and 2 Peter 1:10   a. Diligently
   h. Psalm 5:3 and 1 Thessalonians 5:17   h. Prayerfully

The Cost of Following the Master

If we are to become true followers or disciples of the Lord Jesus Christ, there are many things that we must give up or lay aside. We must be willing to follow Christ at the expense of human relationships, worldly pleasure, and earthly gain. We must be willing to follow even at the expense of sacrificing our personal desires and physical comfort. Salvation is God's gift to us, at His own expense, but we must willingly bear the cost of discipleship.

4. Use the following verses to examine and discuss the cost of following Christ.
   a) **Human Relationships:**
      - Jesus' Example (Matthew 12:47-50)
      - Jesus left His human family to do the will of His heavenly Father.
      - Abraham's Example (Genesis 22:10-12, 16-18)
      - Abraham was willing to sacrifice his son in faith and obedience to God.
      - Jesus' Teaching (Matthew 10:37-38)
      - Our love relationship with the Master must become more important than any other relationship.
      - Jesus' Promise (Matthew 19:29)
        God will reward our efforts and our sacrifice for Him.
   b) **Worldly Pleasures:**
      - Jesus' Example (Matthew 4:1-11)
      - Jesus chose to obey God's Word rather than yield to

the worldly temptations offered by the devil.
- Moses' Example (Hebrews 11:24-26)
- Moses chose to suffer affliction with the people of
- God over the pleasure and position of the house of Pharaoh.
- Biblical Truth (1 John 2:15-17)
- The world's pleasures are temporary, but God's promises are eternal.
- Jesus' Promise (Luke 12:32)
- God is pleased to give the kingdom to those who follow the Master.

c) **Earthly Possessions:**
- Jesus' Example (Matthew 8:20; 2 Corinthians 8:9)
- Jesus laid aside His glory and power and was crucified for us so that we might live.
- Paul's Example (Philippians 3:7-8)
- Paul was willing to loose all in order to gain Christ.
- Jesus' Teaching (Matthew 6:19-21, 16:26)
- One soul is more valuable than all of the temporary treasures of this world.
- Biblical Truth (Philippians 4:19)
- God will supply all our needs according to His riches in glory by Christ Jesus.

d) **Personal Comfort:**
- Jesus' Example (Philippians 2:8)
- Jesus humbled Himself and gave His life for us.
- Paul's Example (Acts 21:12-13; Romans 8:18)
- Paul willingly suffered and died for the sake of the Gospel of Jesus Christ.
- Jesus' Teaching (Matthew 16:24-25)
- To come after Him, we must deny ourselves (choose His will and His way), take up our cross (be willing to suffer for His sake), and follow Him (by living in obedience to His Word).
- Biblical Truth (2 Corinthians 4:17; 1 Peter 5:10)
  When we suffer for Christ, God Himself will perfect, strengthen, and establish us.

The Benefits of Following the Master

"How can I repay the Lord for all his goodness to me? I will lift up the cup of salvation and call on the name of the Lord. I will fulfill my vows to the Lord in the presence of all his people" (Psalm 116:12-14, NIV).

5. Match the following Scripture references with the ways that we benefit from following the Master.

a. Isaiah 28:16	b. God's Guidance
b. Psalm 32:8	e. Perfect Peace
c. John 6:47	h. Spiritual Growth
d. John 8:36	g. Heavenly Help
e. John 14:27	d. Freedom from Sin
f. Hebrews 4:9-10	a. Supernatural Security
g. Hebrews 4:16	f. Rest and Refreshment
h. 2 Peter 3:18	c. Everlasting Life

LIFE APPLICATION

Personal Application

1. Evaluate your own response to the call of the Master. Spiritually, are you:
    Still preparing the nets?
    Leaving the boat?
    Sitting at the tax collector's booth?
    Following hard after Jesus?
    Feeling left behind?

2. We must not become forgetful hearers. Make a commitment to pray and read God's Word. Each day this week, ask God: "What is Your will for me today?" Then do whatever He says. Remember that He has a plan for your life. However, you must listen and obey in order to follow in step with Him.

3. Meditate on the following Scripture:
"Brethren, I count not myself to have apprehended: but this one thing I do, forgetting those things which are behind, and reaching forth unto those things which are before, I press toward the mark for the prize of the high calling of God in Christ Jesus" (Philippians 3:13-14)
Look up some of the words to be sure that you understand their meanings. Then commit these verses to memory and apply them in your life.

4. Examine your own life. Do you have:
   Sins to repent?
   People to forgive?
   Past events to forget?
   Obstacles to press past?

5. Determine today that you will fulfill the purpose of your high calling. Remember, as you follow the Master, you can trust Him to meet your needs. He has promised give you "all things that pertain to life and godliness" (2 Peter 1:3).

Church Ministry Application
1. Compare how well your congregation measures up to God's purposes for His people.
   - Is God's voice being heard from the pulpit, the Sunday School lessons, and the Bible Study classes? Is the Word of God being preached and taught?
   - Are people hearing and answering the call of salvation? Is the body of believers united in the love of Christ?

2. Evaluate the direction of the ministry.
   - Are the members of the congregation growing in the grace and the knowledge of our Lord and Saviour Jesus Christ?
   - Is there a well-defined vision for the ministry? (Proverbs 29:18)
   - Are the members "doers" of the Word? How active are the outreach ministries, the ministry of helps, the missions organizations, etc.?

3. Finally, ask God to give you creative ideas to encourage others as they follow Christ.

SESSION TWO

BY THE WORD YOU ARE EQUIPPED

For sessions of 90 minutes or more, use the lesson format for PART ONE and PART TWO.

PART ONE

ACTIVITY	TIME
Opening Prayer	5 minutes
Scripture Search	15 minutes
Chapter Highlights	15 minutes

PART TWO

ACTIVITY	TIME
Small Group Study	15 minutes
Large Group Presentations	20 minutes
Large Group Discussion	10 minutes
Closing Prayer	5 minutes

For sessions of less than 90 minutes, use PART ONE only and assign the Bible Study Application questions as homework.

Lesson Aims: At the end of this two-part Bible study session, the participants should be able to: a) explain the dual nature of the Word of God; b) understand how the Word operates in the lives of believers; c) recognize the importance of diligently studying, applying, and obeying the Word so that they can become spiritually equipped to follow the Master.

PART ONE

A. OPENING PRAYER

Open the session with prayer. Include the requests that God would bless each participant to:
- Understand the nature and the importance of the Word of God.
- Effectively use the Word of God to win life's spiritual battles.
- Become equipped to please God by living according to His Word.

B. SCRIPTURE SEARCH

1. Ask someone to read Matthew 4:1-11 aloud to the group.

By the Word You Are Equipped **21**

2. Use the following statements and questions to review the facts from this Scripture passage:
    a) Describe Jesus' physical condition in this account of Scripture.
        Jesus had fasted for 40 days. At the time of this encounter with the devil, He was in an extreme state of hunger, thirst, and physical weakness.

    b) Why was Jesus in the wilderness?
        Jesus was led by the Spirit into the wilderness. Jesus was in the will of God; He was following the leadership of the Holy Spirit. This event was part of God's plan for His life.

    c) Did God protect Jesus from temptation?
        God allowed the devil to tempt Jesus. Satan tempted Jesus to do evil, but God permitted it for our good that through Jesus' victory we might also become victorious.

    d) How did Jesus win His encounter with the devil?
        Jesus defeats the devil with the written Word of God.

    e) When do the angels come?
        The angels come to minister to Jesus after the devil had left Him.

3. Explain why this account is significant for us today. This biblical record illustrates:
    - An Account of Spiritual Warfare
      In this passage, we see the Word made flesh speaking the written Word and winning the encounter with the devil in the wilderness. Jesus is in fact doing battle with the devil.
    - The Weapon that Defeats Temptation
      Even in His extremely weakened state, Jesus was equipped for battle. The Word of God was the spiritual weapon that Jesus used to defeat the enemy.
    - An Example for Believers
      Although Jesus is the Word incarnate, He laid aside His deity to live on earth as the Son of Man. Jesus faces the devil with the same spiritual weapons which are available to us today, and He wins.

4. Have the participants notice what Jesus **does not** do.
   - In this spiritual battle, Jesus does not use His **natural** abilities.
     He does not look at or consider the temptation which He is offered.
     He does not consider His own feelings or emotions.
     He does not use human reasoning or logic to deal with the devil.
   - In this spiritual battle, Jesus does not use His **supernatural** abilities.
     He does not call on the angels to come to His assistance.
     He does not use His divine power to overcome the enemy.

5. Finally, explain that like Jesus, we too can rely on the sword of the Spirit which is the written Word of God to defeat the strategies of the devil.

6. End the discussion by asking a volunteer to read 2 Corinthians 10:3-5 aloud to the group.

C. CHAPTER HIGHLIGHTS

Using the content of Chapter Two as background, give a general overview of the chapter. Be sure to include the following topics:
1. The Person of Jesus: The Word Made Flesh
2. The Bible: God's Written Word
3. The Work of the Word in the Lives of Believers
4. Becoming Spiritually Equipped with the Word of God

PART TWO

A. BIBLE STUDY APPLICATION

1. Introduction

The Bible Study Application section contains eight questions which provide an opportunity to examine how the Word of God equips us to follow the Master. The discussion of the Bible Study Application questions should confirm that the students understand the importance of Scripture.

Allow as much time as necessary to encourage the exchange of ideas and insights. Use the information preceding each set of questions to help introduce or close the discussion of a topic. Use the Bible verses to help keep the discussion on track. Depending on the size and personality of the group, you can discuss as many or as few of the questions as needed.

2. **Procedure**
Select Small Group Leaders. Ask for volunteers or select three small group leaders. Then assign each small group leader a number from 1-3. (This can also be done beforehand to save time.) Ask the small group leaders to write their numbers on large sheets of white paper so that they can be seen from a distance.

Divide into Small Groups. Inform the participants that they will be separated into small groups. Each group will study a different set of questions and then will present their findings to the larger group at the end of the study period. The questions should be assigned as follows:
- Group #1: Understanding the Word (questions 1-2)
- Group #2: Equipped by the Word (questions 3-4)
- Group #3: Effectively Using the Word (questions 5-8)

Allow Participants to Count Off by Threes. Then ask them to follow the small group leader who is holding their assigned number. Identify the location of each group. (These locations can also be pre-printed on a sheet of paper, photocopied, and distributed to save time.) Participants should then assemble into smaller groups in their respective meeting areas.

B. SMALL GROUP STUDY
1. Small Group Leaders
   Each group will have one topic to explore. For each topic, there are questions and related Scripture references to stimulate discussion.

2. Sharing Insights
   After 15 minutes, designate someone who will summarize the small group discussion within the larger body of participants. Remind the designated person that she or he will only have five minutes to present.

C. LARGE GROUP PRESENTATIONS
Reconvene the Group. Call the small groups back together.

Explain the Procedure. Explain that a representative of each small group will share that group's reflections on the Bible Study Application questions with the larger group.

Remind Small Group Representatives of the Time. Remind each group representative that he or she should try to summarize the group's discussion in five minutes. Allow up to five minutes to discuss each group's presentation.

D. LIFE APPLICATION DISCUSSION*

If time permits, the larger group can then discuss the Personal Application and Church Ministry questions together.

1. Introduction

The Personal Application section contains two multi-part questions which encourage the participants to consider the teaching in light of their own lives. The Church Ministry Application section contains three questions which address some implications for the congregation as a whole.

2. Sharing Insights

This discussion should be open-ended and voluntary. The sharing of personal insights or recommendations for church ministry should be encouraged but not required. The group may have quite a bit to say. Watch the clock! Stop them after 10 minutes.

*Answers are not provided for the Personal Application and Church Ministry sections because of the personal or specific nature of the questions.

E. PREPARATION FOR NEXT MEETING

Assignment. Have the participants read Chapter Three, "You Are Invited" and review the questions in preparation for next week's session. Encourage them to come to the next session prepared to share their insights on the content of the chapter.

You may also want to assign small groups or particular questions to facilitate next week's meeting time.

F. CLOSING PRAYER

Hold hands, form a circle, and ask for specific prayer requests. Then ask for several volunteers to pray, keeping the prayer requests in mind.

ANSWERS TO BIBLE STUDY APPLICATION

Understanding the Word

Two expressions of the Word of God are revealed in Scripture:
- The Person of Jesus: The Word Made Flesh
- The Bible: God's Written Word

1. Use the verses below to explore what the Bible says about Jesus as the Word of God.
   a) Describe the Jesus' relationship with God in the beginning. (John 1:1-2; Colossians 1:15; 1 John 5:7)
   Jesus Christ was preexistent with God in heaven before the creation of the world. Like the Father, He is divine ("the Word was God"). He is also distinct from the Father as the second Person of the Trinity and one with the Father as a member of the Godhead.

   b) Describe the Jesus' relationship to the world. (John 1:3; Colossians 1:16-17; Hebrews 1:1-2)
   Jesus Christ is the Creator and Sustainer of the world.

   c) Describe the Jesus' relationship with humankind. (John 1:14; Matthew 1:23; Galatians 4:4; Hebrews 2:14)
   Jesus, the Word of God who was God, left heaven and became a man and dwelt among us. He exchanged deity for humanity, lived a sinless life on earth, and died on the cross to bring salvation to us.

   d) What does Jesus say about Himself and His relationship with God? (John 8:58; 10:30; 16:15; 17:5, 21-24)
   Jesus Christ also affirms His own divinity. He states that He was with God in the beginning and that He and the Father are one and share all things in common.

2. Use the verses below to explore what the Bible, God's written Word, says about itself.
   a) "Inspired" comes from the Greek word meaning "God-breathed." What does 2 Timothy 3:16 say about the Scriptures? (Check the correct answer.)
   _____ Some of the Bible is inspired by God.
   _____ All of the Bible is inspired by God.
   _____ Only the New Testament is inspired by God.
   _____ Only the parts that speak to you are inspired by God.

b) How was the written Word of God given to us? (2 Peter 1:20-21)
Not by the will of man, but by holy men of God who were moved by the Holy Spirit.

c) How long will the Word of God last? (Isaiah 40:8; Matthew 24:34-35; Luke 21:33; 1 Peter 1:24-25)
The Word of God will last forever.

d) Describe the relationship of the Word of God to spiritual truth. (Numbers 23:19; Psalm 119:151-152; John 17:17)
God cannot lie. His Word is truth.

e) Who is the central character of the written Word of God? (Luke 24:27, 44; John 5:39, 46; 20:31)
Jesus Christ our Saviour is the central character of the written Word of God.

Equipped by the Word

The Word of God contains the spiritual equipment we need to follow Christ.

3. An analogy explains something by comparing it with something else. Look up the verses below and use them to answer the questions which follow.
   a) Jeremiah 5:14 and 23:29
      - What is God's Word compared with?
        God's Word is compared to a devouring fire and a crushing hammer.
      - What are the functions of these objects?
        A hammer breaks the object it strikes and a fire consumes everything in its way.
      - What does this analogy teach about the Word of God? (See also Isaiah 55:11.)
        God's Word is irresistible; it will accomplish what God intends. No obstacle or opposition can stop it.
   b) Matthew 4:4 and 1 Peter 2:2
      - What is God's Word compared with?
        God's Word is compared to milk and bread.
      - What are the functions of these objects?
        Milk and bread are the basic foods. They satisfy hunger

and provide nourishment.
- What does this analogy teach about the Word of God?
  God's Word is spiritual food that supports our spiritual life and growth. We should "hunger" for the Word.

c) Luke 8:11 and 1 Peter 1:23
- What is God's Word compared with?
  God's Word is compared to a seed.
- What is the function of this object?
  A seed contains life. When sown under proper conditions, it grows to produce a mature plant of the same kind. Mature plants bear fruit and seeds which reproduce to provide a harvest.
- What does this analogy teach about the Word of God? (See also Genesis 1:27 and Romans 8:29.)
  God's Word is the spiritual seed that produces a spiritual harvest in our hearts and lives. As we grow spiritually through the Word of God, we become more and more like Jesus Christ.

d) Ephesians 5:26
- What is God's Word compared with?
  God's Word is compared to water.
- What is the function of this object?
  Water can be used to wash or clean objects.
- What does this analogy teach about, the Word of God? (See also Psalm 51:10 and 119:9, 11.)
  The Word of God exposes sinfulness and reveals truth. As we apply and obey the Word, our hearts and lives become spiritually clean.

4. Match the following verses with the spiritual equipment that God's Word gives us.

   a. Joshua 1:8-9   f. Spiritual Wisdom
   b. 2 Timothy 3:16   b. Sound Doctrine
   c. 2 Timothy 3:17   e. Divine Direction
   d. Romans 15:4   a. Good Success
   e. Psalm 32:8 and 119:105   c. Good Works
   f. Matthew 7:24 and Colossians 3:16   d. Heavenly Hope
   g. Philippians 2:16 and 1 John 5:13   g. Eternal Life

28 In Step With the Master

Effectively Using the Word

It is not enough to have the right spiritual equipment, we must also be able to use it. To effectively use the God's Word, we must first know it and then do it.

5. Match the following verses with the actions we must take to effective use the Word of God.

   a. Joshua 1:8　　　　　e. Hear it
   b. Psalm 78:5-7　　　　g. Read it
   c. Psalm 119:11　　　　d. Study it
   d. 2 Timothy 2:15　　　b. Teach it
   e. Romans 10:17　　　 f. Do it
   f. James 1:22　　　　　c. Memorize it
   g. Revelation 1:3　　　 a. Meditate on it

6. Use the verses in question 5 to answer the following questions.
   a) Why should we hear the Word?
      To increase our faith in God.
   b) Why should we read the Word?
      To be blessed.
   c) Why should we study the Word?
      To receive God's approval.
   d) Why should we teach the Word?
      To cause others to set their hope on the Lord, to remember His works, and to keep His commandments.
   e) Why should we become doers of the Word?
      To avoid deceiving ourselves.
   f) Why should we memorize the Word?
      To avoid sin and keep our lives pure.
   g) Why should we meditate on the Word?
      To make our way prosperous and to have good success.

7. Ezra was a man who effectively used the Word of God. Read Ezra 7:10 and answer the following questions.
   a) What did Ezra do?
      Ezra had devoted himself to study and obey the Word of God and to teach it to others.

b) What we can learn from the order of his actions?
We can learn to apply the Scriptures to our own lives before we teach them to others.

8. The Jewish believers at Berea effectively used the Word of God. Read Acts 17:10-11 and answer the following questions.
    a) What did the Berean Christians do?
    The Bereans received the Word with eagerness and searched the Scriptures daily to see whether Paul and Silas were preaching the truth.
    b) What we can learn from their actions?
    We can learn not only to be ready to hear and receive the Word that is preached to us, but also to check the Scriptures for ourselves to confirm the truth of what we have heard.

LIFE APPLICATION

Personal Application
1. Consider following questions in light of Jesus' example in Matthew 4:1-11.
    - What kinds of hard times have you faced lately?
    - How have you responded to them?
    - Have you ever felt that as a Christian you should be protected from temptations and trails?
    - Read 1 Corinthians 10:13. Consider how you can adjust your perspective according to Word of God when in the midst of tough times.

2. Decide to effectively apply the Word of God.
    - List some or the areas of your life where you are facing challenges or difficulty.
    - Use a topical Bible to find the commandments, instructions, or promises in God's Word which address these areas. (Where there are no specific Scriptures, find out what scriptural principles apply.)
    - Write the Scriptures on a card or piece of paper that you can carry with you.
    - Memorize and meditate on these Scriptures so that you can become equipped to walk in victory.

Church Ministry Application
1. How can the members of the congregation be encouraged to witness to others and invite them to church to hear the Word of God?

2. Evaluate the children's ministry. Are the children encouraged to study and memorize the Word of God? Are they learning the Word through creative ways such as songs, games, and stories? Can they recite simple biblical principles?

3. It has been said that 20% of the congregation usually does 80% of the work. Does this saying seem true for your church? How can the members be encouraged to become doers of the Word?

SESSION THREE

YOU ARE INVITED

For sessions of 90 minutes or more, use the lesson format for PART ONE and PART TWO.

PART ONE

ACTIVITY	TIME
Opening Prayer	5 minutes
Scripture Discussion	20 minutes
Chapter Highlights	15 minutes

PART TWO

ACTIVITY	TIME
Small Group Study	20 minutes
Large Group Presentations	20 minutes
Large Group Discussion	10 minutes
Closing Prayer	5 minutes

For sessions of less than 90 minutes, use PART ONE only and assign the Bible Study Application questions as homework.

Lesson Aims: At the end of this two-part Bible study session, the participants should be able to: a) describe importance of repentance, the Gospel of Jesus Christ, and the Great Commission; b) consider the benefits of accepting and the consequences of rejecting God's offer of salvation; c) understand their responsibility to extend God's divine invitation of salvation through Jesus Christ to others.

Preparation: Write or type the following numbered statements on a sheet of paper. Then use scissors to separate the statements. (Each statement should be on a separate piece of paper.)

1. Everybody's doing it!
2. What will people think?
3. I might as well. You know, just in case.
4. I AM IMPORTANT. Move over, make room for me.
5. I am religious. I should be first.
6. I am ABOVE all of this.

But I'll do it anyway, just to show
how humble I REALLY am.
7. Read Matthew 3:1-6 aloud
8. Read Matthew 3:7-10 aloud
9. Read Matthew 3:11-12 aloud

Use a paper clip to keep the statements together and bring them to class.

PART ONE

A. OPENING PRAYER

Open the session with prayer. Include the requests that God would bless each participant to:

- Realize the importance of repentance.
- Become committed to inviting others to become believers in Jesus Christ.
- Understand the consequences of refusing to believe the Gospel of Jesus Christ.

B. SCRIPTURE DISCUSSION

The Scripture Reading and Scripture Search sections for this Bible study lesson are combined in an orchestrated dialogue with the class.

1. Ask for volunteers to help with the Scripture Discussion.

2. Distribute all of the printed statements. If there are fewer than nine volunteers, give two statements to some of the participants. Ask those who receive Scripture references to look them up and be prepared to read those verses from their Bibles.

3. Inform the class that you will be conducting an orchestrated dialogue or role play. Explain that you will hold up your fingers to indicate when the volunteers are to stand up and read their numbered statements aloud. Encourage them to have fun, use body language, and read with feeling when their turn comes.

4. Then begin the dialogue.
- Have you ever gone to a party just to make an appearance or to see who was there? Or have you ever accepted an invitation with an ulterior motive, other than to join the celebration?

If so, then you may be able to understand why many of the Pharisees and Sadducees came to John to be baptized.

For example, some of them may have said:

- *(Hold up one finger, as volunteer # 1 reads)*
  "Everybody's doing it!"

- *(Hold up two fingers, as volunteer # 2 reads)*
  "What will people think?"

- *(Hold up three fingers, as volunteer # 3 reads)*
  "I might as well. You know, just in case."

Or others probably said:

- *(Hold up four fingers, as volunteer # 4 reads)*
  "I AM IMPORTANT. Move over, make room for me."

- *(Hold up five fingers, as volunteer # 5 reads)*
  "I am religious. I should be first."

- *(Hold up six fingers, as volunteer # 6 reads)*
  "I am ABOVE all of this. But I'll do it anyway, just to show how humble I REALLY am."

But the Word of God says:
- The Lord does not look at things the way we do. Man looks on the outward appearance, but God sees the heart (1 Samuel 16:7b, paraphrased).

- When God extends His divine invitation to us, He judges our response by looking first at our hearts and then at our actions.

5. Use the following information to describe the Pharisees and the Sadducees:
   - The Pharisees and the Sadducees were two of the

most prominent Jewish religious groups of their day.

- The **Pharisees** adhered to all of the Old Testament law and their own human interpretations of it. They proudly practiced religion as an outward form only, with no inward reverence or purity of heart.

- The **Sadducees,** while appearing to religiously keep the Old Testament law, really denied many of its teachings. Their lives were immoral and worldly.

6. Then continue the dialogue.
    - In Matthew chapter 3, John the Baptist extended God's divine invitation to repent and be baptized.

    - *(Hold up seven fingers, as volunteer # 7 reads the Scripture passage)* Matthew 3:1-6

    - However, the hearts of the Pharisees were still hard. They showed no evidence of a change of mind. They showed no evidence of a change of ways. When they responded in pride to God's invitation to repent, John the Baptist rebuked them strongly.

    - *(Hold up eight fingers, as volunteer # 8 reads the Scripture passage)* Matthew 3:7-10

    - As Jesus' forerunner, John pointed ahead. He pointed to Jesus' power, to Jesus' baptism, and to Jesus' divine ability to separate true believers from pretenders and deal with them accordingly.

    - *(Hold up nine fingers, as volunteer # 9 reads the Scripture passage)* Matthew 3:11-12

7. Conclude the dialogue by reminding the participants that:
    Genuine repentance and true faith in Jesus Christ begins as a matter of the heart. However, it must also be evident by lives that forsake sin and produce good fruit.

C. CHAPTER HIGHLIGHTS
Before discussing the chapter, review the following terms:

Repentance—Turning from sin; a change of mind that brings with it a change of direction and behavior.

God's Divine Invitation— The Good News of the Gospel of Jesus Christ; God's offer of salvation to all who will repent from sin and turn to Him through faith in Jesus Christ.

Using the content of Chapter Three as background, give a general overview of the chapter. Be sure to include the following topics:
1. A Divine Invitation
2. We Are Called to Invite Others
3. The Purpose of the Invitation
4. Why Some May Refuse to Respond
5. The Consequences of Rejecting God's Invitation
6. The Benefits of Accepting God's Invitation

PART TWO

A. BIBLE STUDY APPLICATION
1. Introduction

The Bible Study Application section contains eight questions which provide an opportunity to examine our invitation to follow the Master. The discussion of the Bible Study Application questions should confirm that the students understand the importance of receiving and extending God's divine invitation of salvation through Jesus Christ.

Allow as much time as necessary to encourage the exchange of ideas and insights. Use the information preceding each set of questions to help introduce or close the discussion of a topic. Use the Bible verses to help keep the discussion on track. Depending on the size and personality of the group, you can discuss as many or as few of the questions as needed.

2. Procedure

Select Small Group Leaders. Ask for volunteers or select two small group leaders. Then assign a number to each small group leader. (This can also be done beforehand to save time.) Ask the small group leaders to write their numbers on large sheets of white paper so that they can be seen from a distance.

Divide into Small Groups. Inform the participants that they will be separated into two groups. Each group will study a different set of questions and then will present their findings to the larger group at the end of the study period. The questions should be assigned as follows:

> Group #1: We Are Invited to Repent from Sin (questions 1-5)
>
> Group #2: We Are Invited to Share the Gospel of Jesus Christ (questions 6-10)

Divide the Bible Study Group in Half. Then ask them to follow the small group leader who is holding their assigned number. Identify the location of each group. (These locations can also be pre-printed on a sheet of paper, photocopied, and distributed to save time.) Participants should then assemble into smaller groups in their respective meeting areas.

B. SMALL GROUP STUDY

1. Small Group Leaders

Each group will have one topic to explore. For each topic, there are questions and related Scripture references to stimulate discussion.

2. Sharing Insights

After 20 minutes, designate someone who will summarize the small group discussion within the larger body of participants. Remind the designated person that she or he will only have five minutes to present.

C. LARGE GROUP PRESENTATIONS

Reconvene the Group. Call the small groups back together.

Explain the Procedure. Explain that a representative of each small group will share that group's reflections on the Bible Study Application questions with the larger group.

Remind Small Group Representatives of the Time. Remind each group representative that he or she should try to summarize the group's discussion in less than five minutes. Allow up to five minutes to discuss each group's presentation.

D. LIFE APPLICATION DISCUSSION*

If time permits, the larger group can then discuss the Personal Application and Church Ministry questions together.

1. Introduction
   The Personal Application section contains five questions which encourage the participants to consider the teaching in light of their own lives. The Church Ministry Application section contains three questions which address some implications for the congregation as a whole.

2. Sharing Insights
   This discussion should be open-ended and voluntary. The sharing of personal insights or recommendations for church ministry should be encouraged but not required. The group may have quite a bit to say. Watch the clock! Stop them after 10 minutes.

*Answers are not provided for the Personal Application and Church Ministry sections because of the personal or specific nature of the questions.

E. PREPARATION FOR NEXT MEETING
Assignment. Have the participants read Chapter Four, "You Are Made Whole" and review the questions in preparation for next week's session. Encourage them to come to the next session prepared to share their insights on the content of the chapter.

You may also want to assign small groups or particular questions to facilitate next week's meeting time.

F. CLOSING PRAYER
Hold hands, form a circle, and ask for specific prayer requests. Then ask for several volunteers to pray, keeping the prayer requests in mind.

ANSWERS TO BIBLE STUDY APPLICATION

We Are Invited to Repent from Sin
We must clearly understand the importance of repentance.
- Repentance precedes forgiveness. Before we can truly turn to God, we must first turn away from sin.
- Repentance is a matter of the heart which becomes evident by our actions.
- Repentance is a life-long process. Even believers must repent from sin and receive forgiveness so that we may continue to follow the Master.

1. In addition to John the Baptist and our Lord Jesus Christ, use the verses below to answer questions about others who preached repentance from sin.
    a) Acts 26:20
        - Who was preaching?
          Paul was preaching.
        - What did he preach?
          Paul preached that people should repent and turn to God.
        - To whom was he preaching?
          Paul was preaching to the Jews in Damascus, in Jerusalem, in all Judea, and to all the Gentiles also. In other words, Paul was preaching to everyone.
        - How would they prove their repentance?
          Paul said that they would prove their repentance by their deeds.

    b) Acts 2:37-39
        - Who was preaching?
          Peter was preaching.
        - What did he preach?
          Peter preached that people should repent and be baptized in the name of Jesus Christ to receive forgiveness of sins.
        - To whom was he was preaching?
          Peter was preaching to the present generation who would hear and believe in Christ; to their children, the next generation; and to all who were far off, the third and subsequent generations. In other words, the message was for all who would hear and answer God's call throughout the ages.
        - What was the promise?
          Peter preached that they would not only receive forgiveness of sins, but also God's gift of the Holy Spirit.

2. Use the following verses to examine God's promises to those who will repent.
    a) 1 John 1:9
        - What is the condition?
          We must confess our sins.
        - What is God's promise?

God will be faithful and just to forgive our sins and cleanse us from all unrighteousness.
  b) Acts 3:19
     - What is the condition?
       We must repent and become converted.
     - What is God's promise?
       Our sins will be blotted out and we will be refreshed in the presence of God.

3. Why is repentance necessary? (Isaiah 59:2; Romans 3:23; 6:23; Luke 13:3)
   Sin separates us from God. Without Christ, we all are guilty of sin. Unless we repent from sin and turn to God, we will perish.

4. Why is repentance important? (Acts 17:30-31; 2 Corinthians 7:10)
   True repentance is the first step to salvation. We are therefore commanded to repent because God will judge everyone.

5. How is true repentance demonstrated? (Matthew 7:15-21; 1 John 3:10)
   A repentant heart is demonstrated by our actions. If we have truly turned from sin to salvation in Jesus Christ, our actions will show our obedience to God's Word and our love for Him.

We Are Invited to Share the Gospel of Jesus Christ
As believers, we have Good News. Each day God extends an open invitation to every living person to repent from sin and receive salvation. However, all around us there are neighbors, coworkers, friends, and loved ones who have not accepted God's invitation. As God's people, we must make His offer of salvation known to others. Every believer is called to share the Gospel and to invite others to receive salvation through Jesus Christ.

6. Read 1 Corinthians 15:1-4, 17-22. Use these passages and the related Scriptures below to answer questions about the Gospel of Jesus Christ.
  a) Once we have received the Gospel, what should we do? (vv. 1-2; Hebrews 3:14; 10:23)
     We are to keep our salvation through Jesus Christ in mind, to stand in God's grace, and to hold fast our confident faith in Christ.
  b) List the main points of the Gospel. (vv. 3-4; Luke 24:45-46; Acts 26:22-23)

The Gospel of Jesus Christ is the Good News that Jesus died for our sins according to the Scriptures. And that He was buried and rose again according to the Scriptures.

   c) What does Paul mean by the phrase "according to the Scriptures"? (vv. 3-4; Isaiah 53:1-12; John 5:39)
The Gospel of salvation was foretold by Moses and the prophets. Jesus fulfilled every Scripture concerning His life, death, and resurrection. He made salvation available to those who believe in and follow Him.

   d) Why is Christ's resurrection an important part of the Gospel? (vv. 17-22)
Christ's resurrection confirms our hope of eternal life.

7. Jesus left instructions for us. Read the following verses and use them to answer the questions below.

   a) Mark 16:15-16
- Where are we to go?
  We are to go into all the world.
- To whom are we to preach?
  We are to preach to all creation.
- What does Jesus promise?
  Jesus promises that those who believe and are baptized will be saved, but those who do not believe will be damned.

   b) Matthew 28:19-20
- What are we to do?
  We are to go and make disciples of all nations, baptizing them in the name of the Father and of the Son and of the Holy Spirit, and teaching them to obey the Word of God.
- What does Jesus promise?
  Jesus promises to be with us always, even to the end of the world.

   c) Luke 24:45-49
- What does Jesus do first?
  Jesus reminds them of what the Scriptures said concerning His suffering and resurrection.
- What are we to do?

We preach repentance and remission of sins in the name of Christ to all nations.
- What does Jesus promise?
Jesus promises that we will be given the Holy Spirit and power from on high.

8. Match the following verses with the ways that we should communicate the Gospel to others.

a. Romans 1:16	g.	Earnestly
b. 1 Corinthians 4:1-2	a.	Unashamedly
c. 1 Corinthians 9:19	h.	Readily
d. Ephesians 4:15	f.	Graciously
e. Ephesians 6:19-20	d.	Lovingly
f. Colossians 4:6	c.	Humbly
g. 1 Peter 3:15	b.	Faithfully
h. Jude 3	e.	Boldly

9. Match the following verses with some biblical methods used to communicate the Gospel to others. (Answers may be used more than once.)

a. Personal Testimony

b. The Samaritan Woman and Her Townspeople—John 4:28-30

a. The Blind Man and the Pharisees—John 9:10-11

b. Public Invitation

d. Phillip and the Ethiopian Eunuch—Acts 8:35-37

c. Godly Lifestyle

d Paul and Silas and the Keeper of the Prison—Acts 16:30-32

c. Wives and Unsaved Husbands—1 Peter 3:1

d. Preaching the Gospel

10. Use the verses below to review what the Bible says about those who confess Christ.
  a) If we confess Christ what will Jesus do? (Luke 12:8)
  Jesus will confess us before the angels.

b) If we confess Christ and believe that God raised Him from the dead, what will happen to us? (Romans 10:9)
We shall be saved.
c) Who will receive glory when we reverence the name of Jesus Christ and confess that He is Lord? (Philippians 2:11)
God will receive glory.
d) What promise is made to those who confess that Jesus is the Son of God? (1 John 4:15)
God will dwell with us, and we will dwell in God.

LIFE APPLICATION

Personal Application

1. List the names of neighbors, coworkers, friends, and loved ones who have not accepted God's invitation of salvation through Jesus Christ. Pray for them, and look for opportunities to share the Good News with them this week. Remember, tomorrow is not promised to anyone.

2. You should always be ready to give an answer to anyone who asks about your hope in Christ (1 Peter 3:15, paraphrased). This week, take the time to consider and write down the following information:
- A brief testimony of how you were saved
- A clear statement of the Gospel of Jesus Christ
- An outline of how to receive salvation through Jesus Christ

3. Practice sharing your faith by asking a family member to role play different situations with you.

4. Develop questions to help direct the conversation toward the Gospel without putting pressure on others. Read the suggestions below, then add some of your own.
- Are you interested in spiritual things?
- Have you ever thought about becoming a Christian?
- Do you think a person can have peace in today's world?

5. Finally, remember that the power of salvation is not in us. We are to simply share the Gospel and invite others to receive salvation through Jesus Christ. However, as Christ's ambassadors on earth, let us also be careful to represent Him well to others (2 Corinthians 5:20).

Church Ministry Application

1. We live in an immoral society. Although Christians may sin, we should not practice sin. How often is the necessity of repentance preached in your church?

2. The Great Commission to go and make disciples has been given to all believers.
> What emphasis is placed on evangelism?
> Are there training programs for the members of the congregation?
> Is there an outreach ministry in the community?
> What can be done to improve the effectiveness of this critical church mission?

3. We must not neglect our responsibility to share the Good News of the Gospel at home.
> How often is the Gospel preached from the pulpit?
> How often are people invited to receive salvation through Jesus Christ?
> How often are the members encouraged to bring their unsaved friends and family to church?
> Are there programs designed to reach those who are not saved (e.g. a Super Bowl fellowship, a Hallelujah Party to replace a Halloween Party, parenting classes, plays, musicals, etc.)? If not, consider what type of event might work well in your congregation. Make a suggestion and offer your service.

SESSION FOUR

YOU ARE MADE WHOLE

For sessions of 90 minutes or more, use the lesson format for PART ONE and PART TWO.

PART ONE

ACTIVITY	TIME
Opening Prayer	5 minutes
Scripture Search	10 minutes
Chapter Highlights	25 minutes

PART TWO

ACTIVITY	TIME
Small Group Study	15 minutes
Large Group Presentations	20 minutes
Large Group Discussion	10 minutes
Closing Prayer	5 minutes

Lesson Aims: At the end of this two-part Bible study session, the participants should be able to: a) explain the significance of the Sabbath rest; b) understand that Jesus came to bring wholeness to every area of our lives.

PART ONE

A. OPENING PRAYER

Open the session with prayer. Include the requests that God would bless each participant to:
- Submit every broken or wounded place in their hearts and lives to the Great Physician.
- Understand the Jesus Christ is the same yesterday, today, and forever.
- Experience Christ's healing power in every area of their lives.

B. SCRIPTURE SEARCH

1. Ask someone to read Luke 6:6-11 aloud to the group.

2. Ask for volunteers to answer the following questions:
    - In what place did these events occur?
      In the synagogue.
    - Why were the scribes and Pharisees watching Jesus?
      They wanted to see if Jesus would heal someone on the Sabbath day.
    - What is the one question Jesus asked the onlookers?
      "Is it lawful on the Sabbath days to do good, or to do evil?" (Luke 6:9).
    - After looking around at all of them, what did Jesus say to the man?
      "Stretch forth thy hand"(Luke 6:10).
    - When the man obeyed, what happened?
      His withered hand was restored as whole as the other.
    - Instead of rejoicing or praising God in the synagogue, how did the scribes and Pharisees respond?
      They were filled with madness (enraged) and discussed what they might do to Jesus.

C. CHAPTER HIGHLIGHTS

Before discussing the chapter, define the following terms:

Scribes—Also called "teachers of the Law." Learned men of their day who copied or transcribed Scripture. As legal experts trained to teach and apply Old Testament law, they were obsessed with the accuracy of Scripture even down to the "jot" and "tittle" (the two smallest consonant forms in the Hebrew alphabet). The chief priests and the scribes together made up the Sanhedrin (the Jewish Senate and Supreme Court). This body was in charge of the civil and religious affairs of the Jews and were given considerable authority under Roman rule.

Sabbath—A day of rest from labor. God created the world in six days and set aside the seventh day for rest. He then established the Sabbath rest as a pattern for humankind. Christians later changed their day of rest to the first day of the week—the day of Christ's resurrection—and named it Sunday.

Jewish Synagogue—The Jewish center for religious worship; similar to a Christian church. Places of worship which appear in the Bible include: the altar (Abraham), the tabernacle (Moses), the Temple at Jerusalem (David and Solomon), synagogues (Jews), and churches (Christians).

Wholeness—A state of being healthy, sound, well, healed, not broken or fractured, entire, or complete.

Bible Background: The Sabbath Rest
1. Review the institution of the Sabbath.
   - Ask a volunteer to read Genesis 2:2-3 aloud.
   - Then ask another volunteer to read Exodus 20:8-11 aloud.
   - Point out that this is the fourth of the Ten Commandments that God gave to Moses on Mount Sinai.

2. Emphasize the wisdom of observing the Sabbath rest.
   - Ask the participants why they think a Sabbath day of rest was commanded by God.
   - Explain that: By design, God ordained a Sabbath rest for humankind. This pattern was established for our benefit. God is our Creator, and He knows what is best and beneficial for His creation.

3. Mention modern sociological studies on the importance of rest.
   - It is well-known that people have suffered shortened life-spans or even death as a result of constant work.
   - Experts have explored the balance of rest and work. Their findings have consistently confirmed the truth of God's Word. No other pattern appears to be as effective as God's system of one day of rest in a seven-day period.

   (For more information, see *The Thompson Chain Reference Bible Companion*, Howard A. Hanke, Indianapolis: B. B. Kirkbride Bible Co., Inc., 1989, pp. 48-49.)

4. Describe the Jewish observance of the Sabbath.
   - In Exodus 20:8, God commanded that His children should remember the Sabbath and keep it holy. However, the true meaning of the Sabbath rest had become clouded.
   - By Jesus' time, keeping the Sabbath involved obeying many oppressive Jewish ordinances. In addition to the written law, Jewish leaders established 613 rules and regulations to govern behavior on the Sabbath. This elaborate system included 365 negative precepts (like the number of days in a year) which defined the things the Jews must not do on the Sabbath, and 248 positive precepts (like the number of bones in the body) which listed the things that Jews must do on the Sabbath.

   (For more information, see *The Thompson Chain Reference Bible Companion*, p. 143.)
   - To summarize, ask someone to read John 5:16 aloud to the group.

5. Discuss Jesus' example and teachings concerning the Sabbath.
   - Point out that it was Jesus' custom to worship God in the synagogue on the Sabbath day (Luke 4:16).
   - However, the scribes and the Pharisees who enforced the letter of the law came into direct conflict with Jesus.
   - Ask a volunteer to read Mark 2:27 aloud to the group.
   - Ask the class what they think Jesus meant by this statement.
   - Then, ask them to state in their own words what they think was really going on between Jesus and the scribes and Pharisees in Luke 6:6-11. Encourage the class to discuss the Pharisees' motives and Jesus' objectives in this encounter. Use this discussion to confirm their understanding of the Scripture passage.
   - Finally, ask a volunteer to read Luke 6:5 aloud to the group.
   - Discuss the meaning of this truth.

Chapter Discussion
Using the content of Chapter Four as background, give a general overview of the chapter. Be sure to include the following topics:
1. Jesus Can Make Us Whole
2. Who Is Sick?
3. Receiving and Rejecting Jesus' Offer of Wholeness
4. Being Made Whole

PART TWO
A. BIBLE STUDY APPLICATION
1. Introduction

The Bible Study Application section contains eight questions which provide an opportunity to examine our invitation to follow the Master. The discussion of the Bible Study Application questions should confirm that the students understand the importance of being made whole through the power of Jesus Christ.

Allow as much time as necessary to encourage the exchange of ideas and insights. Use the information preceding each set of questions to help introduce or close the discussion of a topic. Use the Bible verses to help keep the discussion on track. Depending on the size and personality of the group, you can discuss as many or as few of the questions as needed.

2. Procedure

Select Small Group Leaders. Ask for volunteers or select three small group leaders. Then assign each small group leader a number from 1-3. (This can also be done beforehand to save time.) Ask the small group leaders to write their numbers on large sheets of white paper so that they can be seen from a distance.

Divide into Small Groups. Inform the participants that they will be separated into small groups. Each group will study a different set of questions and then will present their findings to the larger group at the end of the study period. The questions should be assigned as follows:

        Group #1: Jesus Christ, Our Healer (questions 1-4)
        Group #2: The Importance of Faith (question 5)
        Group #3: You Can Be Made Whole (questions 6-8)

Allow Participants to Count Off by Threes. Then ask them to follow the small group leader who is holding their assigned number. Identify the location of each group. (These locations can also be pre-printed on a sheet of paper, photocopied, and distributed to save time.) Participants should then assemble into smaller groups in their respective meeting areas.

B. SMALL GROUP STUDY

1. **Small Group Leaders**

   Each group will have one topic to explore. For each topic, there are questions and related Scripture references to stimulate discussion.

2. **Sharing Insights**

   After 15 minutes, designate someone who will summarize the small group discussion within the larger body of participants. Remind the designated person that she or he will only have five minutes to present.

C. LARGE GROUP PRESENTATIONS

Reconvene the Group. Call the small groups back together.

Explain the Procedure. Explain that a representative of each small group will share that group's reflections on the Bible Study Application questions with the larger group.

Remind Small Group Representatives of the Time. Remind each group representative that he or she should try to summarize the group's discussion in less than five minutes. Allow up to five minutes to discuss each group's presentation.

D. LIFE APPLICATION DISCUSSION*

If time permits, the larger group can then discuss the Personal Application and Church Ministry questions together.

1. Introduction

The Personal Application section contains two multi-part questions which encourage the participants to consider the teaching in light of their own lives. The Church Ministry Application section contains three questions which address some implications for the congregation as a whole.

2. Sharing Insights

This discussion should be open-ended and voluntary. The sharing of personal insights or recommendations for church ministry should be encouraged but not required. The group may have quite a bit to say. Watch the clock! Stop them after 10 minutes.

*Answers are not provided for the Personal Application and Church Ministry sections because of the personal or specific nature of the questions.

E. PREPARATION FOR NEXT MEETING

Assignment. Have the participants read Chapter Five, "You Have the Authority" and review the questions in preparation for next week's session. Encourage them to come to the next session prepared to share their insights on the content of the chapter.

You may also want to assign small groups or particular questions to facilitate next week's meeting time.

F. CLOSING PRAYER

Hold hands, form a circle, and ask for specific prayer requests. Then ask for several volunteers to pray, keeping the prayer requests in mind.

ANSWERS TO BIBLE STUDY APPLICATION

Jesus Christ, Our Healer

You may have heard people say, "We live in a sin-sick world." However, even in our critical condition, divine help is available. Jesus offers healing to us. He came that we might have life, and that we might have it more abundantly (John 10:10).

1. Read the following Scriptures. Then fill in the blanks to describe the spiritual and physical healing that Jesus provides.
    a) Isaiah 53:5 and 1 Peter 2:24
       Jesus was beaten and broken that we might be **healed.**
    b) Colossians 1:14 and Ephesians 1:7
       Jesus shed His blood that we might be **forgiven.**
    c) Romans 5:19 and 2 Corinthians 5:21
       Jesus who knew no sin, was made to be sin for us; that we might be made **righteous.**

2. Read Luke 4:18-21. Based on this Scripture passage, list six things that Jesus came to earth to do.
    a) Preach the Gospel to the poor.
    b) Heal the broken-hearted.
    c) Preach deliverance to the captives.
    d) Restore sight to the blind.
    e) Set at liberty those who were bruised.
    f) Preach the acceptable year of the Lord.

3. Read Luke 7:22. List six things that Jesus did which demonstrated that He was Christ, the long-awaited Messiah.
    a) He caused the blind to see.
    b) He caused the lame to walk.
    c) He cleansed the lepers.
    d) He caused the deaf to hear.
    e) He raised the dead.
    f) He preached the Gospel to the poor.

4. Read John 14:6; Ephesians 2:18; and 1 Timothy 2:5. According to these verses, what important relationship can Jesus Christ restore?
   Our relationship with God, our Father which was broken by sin can be restored through Jesus Christ our Lord.

The Importance of Faith
Jesus often said "Your faith has made you whole."

5. Use the following verses to examine the importance of faith in receiving Jesus' offer of wholeness.
    a) Read the account of Jesus cleansing the leper from

You Are Made Whole **51**

Mark 1:40-42.
- What did the man say that demonstrated his faith?
  "If you are willing, you can make me clean" (v. 40b, NASB)
- In response to his faith, what did Jesus do?
  Jesus showed compassion and touched him.
- What did Jesus say to the man?
  "I am willing; be cleansed" (v. 41b, NASB)
- What happened?
  Immediately the leprosy left him, and he was healed.
- Why was the leper's faith important?
  Answers will vary.

b) Read the account of Jesus healing the paralyzed man from Mark 2:3-12.
- What did the men do to demonstrate their faith in verses 3-4?
- They used extreme measures to get the paralyzed man into the presence of Jesus.
- In response to their faith, what did Jesus say to the paralytic?
- "My son, your sins are forgiven" (v. 5b, NASB)
  Was this a spiritual or a physical healing?
  The forgiveness of sins is a spiritual healing.
- What do verses 9-10 tell us about Jesus' authority over both physical and spiritual sickness?
  Jesus has all authority and power. He came to bring both physical and spiritual healing to us.
- What else did Jesus say to the paralytic in verse 11?
  "I say to you, rise, take up your pallet and go home" (v. 11, NASB)
- What did the man do?
  He arose and immediately took up his pallet and left.
- Why was the paralyzed man's faith important?
  Answers will vary.

c) Read the account of Jesus healing the centurion's servant from Matthew 8:5-10, 13.
- What did the centurion do to demonstrate his faith in verses 5-6?
  He came to Jesus and asked him to heal his servant.

- What did Jesus say in response to his request?
  "I will come and heal him" (v. 7, NASB)
- How did the centurion respond in verse 8?
  He asked Jesus not to come. The centurion told Jesus that if He would just say the word that his servant would be healed.
- Why did the centurion's explanation of authority reveal?
  It revealed that the centurion's faith in Jesus' word was based on faith in Jesus' divine authority over sickness and disease.
- What was Jesus' response to the centurion's faith in verse 10?
  Jesus marveled.
- What did Jesus say to the centurion in verse 13?
  "Go your way; let it be done to you as you believed" (v. 13, NASB)
- What happened to the servant?
  The servant was healed that hour.
- The centurion was a Roman soldier. Although he was not Jewish, he was a believer. Why was the centurion's faith important?
  Answers will vary.

You Can Be Made Whole

6. There are people who say that Jesus' miracles are "not for us today." Read Hebrews 13:8. In light of this truth and the actions of Jesus described above, what can we conclude?

Jesus Christ, whom we serve and follow, is the same Christ who in His life on earth went about doing good and healing those who were sick. In fact, the Bible says that He will never change. Therefore, we can be confident that He offers healing to us today.

7. Use the following verses to tell why our faith is important.
   a) Mark 11:22
      Jesus instructs His disciples to have faith in God. If we are to follow in step with the Master, we must also have faith in God.
   b) 1 John 5:14
      Our faith is evidence of our confidence in Him. We know that when we ask God in prayer anything according to His will, He hears us.

c) Hebrews 11:6
   Our faith pleases God. In fact, without it we cannot please Him. We must believe that He exists and that He rewards those who diligently seek Him.
   d) Matthew 13:58; Mark 11:24; and James 1:6-7
   Faith is necessary to receive answers to prayer.

8. Read James 5:14-16. Use these verses to answer the following questions.
   a) Why are the sick instructed to call upon those who are in spiritual authority to pray for them? (v. 14; see also Hebrews 13:17)
   As we come to God in faith and submit to the authority that He has ordained, God will answer.
   b) How will God respond to the prayer offered in faith? (v. 15)
   God will restore and heal the physical condition, and if necessary, He will forgive the person's sins and provide spiritual healing.
   c) Why is confession important? (v. 16; see also Proverbs 28:13; 1 John 1:9)
   When we confess our faults to others for prayer, they will know how to pray on our behalf. When we confess our sins, we acknowledge God's authority over us and agree with His Word concerning our behavior. As we come in faith and obedience and ask God for forgiveness, He forgives our sins and cleanses us from all unrighteousness.

LIFE APPLICATION

Personal Application
1. Review the following:
   - Your attitudes
   - Your ambitions
   - Your activities
   - Your associations

   Determine which areas need the healing touch of the Master and bring them to God in prayer. Have faith that He will bring healing and restoration to your life.

2. Review these four areas of life again. Think of some practical way that you can demonstrate spiritual life in each area and do it.

For example:
- In your attitudes: Pick a fruit of the Spirit (Galatians 5:22) and ask God to help you grow in that area this week.
- In your ambitions: Make it your aim to please God this week by walking in the Spirit (Romans 8:8), walking in obedience (1 Thessalonians 4:1), or walking in faith (Hebrews 11:6).
- In your activities: Select a commandment to obey or a scriptural principle to operate by this week (Romans 2:13).
- Your associations: Evaluate the company you keep; not the just with people, but the videos, movies, and musical entertainment as well (2 Corinthians 6:14).

Church Ministry Application

1. Consider the spiritual health of the ministries of your church. Begin to pray faithfully for your spiritual leaders. Consider how you can contribute your time, talents, or treasure to help do the work of the ministry and edify the body of Christ.

2. Consider the physical health of the members of your congregation. Are the sick in the congregation prayed for regularly? Is there a prayer chain for urgent needs? Is there someone that you could visit or send a card of encouragement to today?

3. Jesus faithfully went to the synagogue on the Sabbath to worship God. How can the members of the congregation be encouraged to follow His example? How can the importance of the Sabbath rest be taught and practiced more effectively today?

SESSION FIVE

YOU HAVE THE AUTHORITY

For sessions of 90 minutes or more, use the lesson format for PART ONE and PART TWO.

ACTIVITY	TIME
Opening Prayer	5 minutes
Scripture Search	15 minutes
Chapter Highlights	20 minutes

PART TWO

ACTIVITY	TIME
Small Group Study	15 minutes
Large Group Presentations	25 minutes
Large Group Discussion	15 minutes
Closing Prayer	5 minutes

Lesson Aims: At the end of this two-part Bible study session, the participants should be able to: a) describe Jesus' authority; b) discuss the importance of the name of Jesus; c) understand their responsibility and spiritual authority as believers in Jesus Christ.

PART ONE

A. OPENING PRAYER

Open the session with prayer. Include the requests that God would bless each participant to:
- Realize that Jesus Christ has all power in heaven and earth.
- Understand that as believers, we have been given authority over sin and Satan through Jesus' name.
- Remember that our real reason for rejoicing comes from the truth that we have eternal life through Jesus Christ our Lord.

B. SCRIPTURE SEARCH

1. Ask someone to read Luke 10:1-5 aloud to the group.

2. State that these verses describe the sending out of the 70 disciples. However, some early Bible manuscripts record the number of disciples as 72.

3. Explain that the word **appoint** means "to authoritatively assign and equip for a particular use, task, or office."

4. Ask for volunteers to answer the following questions:
    - Who appointed the men?
      The Lord Jesus Christ.
    - For what task did Jesus appoint them?
      They were appointed to go out and preach the Gospel.
    - Where did Jesus send them?
      Into every city and place.
    - What does the harvest represent?
      People of the world who need to be brought into the kingdom of God.
    - How would you describe the way that Jesus equips them for their appointed task?
      Answers will vary.
      After the opinions are exchanged, be sure to point out the following:
        - Note that they were sent out **without natural protection.** In fact, Jesus said that He was sending them forth as "lambs among wolves."
        - Note that they were sent out **without natural provision.** They were instructed to carry no money, no speeches, no supplies or clothing—not even a change of shoes.
        - Note that they were sent out **without human assistance.** They were to be so intent on their mission that they were not even to exchange social greetings as they went. There was no opportunity to network, gather supporters, or build up the news of their coming by word of mouth. Jesus tells

them to "salute no man by the way."
- Note that they were sent out **without man-made plans.** They had no travel arrangements, hotel reservations, itinerary, or pre-determined destination.
- When they entered a house what were they instructed to do? To first say, "Peace be to this house." The disciples were appointed and equipped to go out in the name of Jesus Christ **with the blessing of peace** for those who would receive them.

5. Ask someone to read Luke 10:17-20 aloud to the group.

6. Explain that these verses describe the return of the disciples. As they obediently went out without natural provision or power, they discovered that they had instead been given supernatural provision and power through the name of Jesus.

7. Ask for volunteers to answer the following questions:
- When they returned, why were they rejoicing?
Because even the devils were subject to them through (or because of) the name of Jesus.
- Instead of rejoicing in their spiritual power, in what does Jesus tell them to rejoice?
They are to rejoice because they have eternal life.

C. CHAPTER HIGHLIGHTS

Using the content of Chapter Five as background, give a general overview of the chapter. Be sure to include the following topics:
1. The Sending
2. The Meaning of Authority
3. The Authority to Harvest
4. The Authority to Pray
5. The Authority to Speak Peace
6. Authority Over the Enemy

PART TWO
A. BIBLE STUDY APPLICATION
1. Introduction

The Bible Study Application section contains seven questions which provide an opportunity to examine our spiritual authority. The discussion of the Bible Study Application questions should confirm that the students understand the authority we have been given as believers in Jesus Christ.

Allow as much time as necessary to encourage the exchange of ideas and insights. Use the information preceding each set of questions to help introduce or close the discussion of a topic. Use the Bible verses to help keep the discussion on track. Depending on the size and personality of the group, you can discuss as many or as few of the questions as needed.

2. Procedure

Select Small Group Leaders. Ask for volunteers or select four small group leaders. Then assign each small group leader a number from 1-4. (This can also be done beforehand to save time.) Ask the small group leaders to write their numbers on large sheets of white paper so that they can be seen from a distance.

Divide into Small Groups. Inform the participants that they will be separated into small groups. Each group will study a different set of questions and then will present their findings to the larger group at the end of the study period. The questions should be assigned as follows:

Group #1: The Authority of Jesus Christ (question 1)
Group #2: The Authority of Jesus' Name (question 2)
Group #3: The Authority of New Testament Believers (questions 3-6)
Group #4: Our Authority in Jesus Christ (question 7)

Allow Participants to Count Off by Fours. Then ask them to follow the small group leader who is holding their assigned number. Identify the location of each group. (These locations can also be pre-printed on a sheet of paper, photocopied, and distributed to save time.) Participants should then assemble into smaller groups in their respective meeting areas.

Note: If the Bible Study is small, divide into three groups and eliminate discussion group #3. You may want to include questions 3-6 as part of the homework assignment.

B. SMALL GROUP STUDY

1. Small Group Leaders

Each group will have one topic to explore. For each topic, there are questions and related Scripture references to stimulate discussion.

2. Sharing Insights

After 15 minutes, designate someone who will summarize the small group discussion within the larger body of participants. Remind the designated person that she or he will only have five minutes to present.

C. LARGE GROUP PRESENTATIONS

Reconvene the Group. Call the small groups back together.

Explain the Procedure. Explain that a representative of each small group will share that group's reflections on the Bible Study Application questions with the larger group.

Remind Small Group Representatives of the Time. Remind each group representative that he or she should try to summarize the group's discussion in less than minutes. Allow up to five minutes to discuss each group's presentation.

D. LIFE APPLICATION DISCUSSION*

If time permits, the larger group can then discuss the Personal Application and Church Ministry questions together.

1. Introduction

The Personal Application section contains three questions which encourage the participants to consider the teaching in light of their own lives. The Church Ministry Application section contains three questions which address some implications for the congregation as a whole.

2. Sharing Insights

This discussion should be open-ended and voluntary. The sharing of personal insights or recommendations for church ministry should be encouraged but not required. The group may have quite a bit to say. Watch the clock! Stop them after 10 minutes.

*Answers are not provided for the Personal Application and Church Ministry sections because of the personal or specific nature of the questions.

60 In Step With the Master

E. PREPARATION FOR NEXT MEETING
Assignment. Have the participants read Chapter Six, "Jesus Will Come for You" and review the questions in preparation for next week's session. Encourage them to come to the next session prepared to share their insights on the content of the chapter.

You may also want to assign small groups or particular questions to facilitate next week's meeting time.

F. CLOSING PRAYER
Hold hands, form a circle, and ask for specific prayer requests. Then ask for several volunteers to pray, keeping the prayer requests in mind.

ANSWERS TO BIBLE STUDY APPLICATION

The Authority of Jesus Christ
The Jewish leaders frequently questioned Jesus saying, "Tell us, by what authority doest thou these things? or who is he that gave thee this authority?" (Luke 20:1-2) Jesus did not answer their questions because He knew their hearts. However, the nature of Jesus' divine authority is revealed in God's Word.

1. Fill in the blanks below to examine what the Word of God tells us about the authority of Jesus Christ.
   a) Matthew 28:18
   > And Jesus came and spake unto them, saying, **All power** is given unto me in heaven and in earth.

   b) John 3:35
   > The Father loveth the Son, and hath given **all things** into his hand.

   c) John 5:26-27
   > For as the Father hath life in himself; so hath he given to the Son to have life in himself; And hath given him authority to **execute judgment** also, because he is the Son of man.

   d) John 17:2
   > As thou hast given him power over **all flesh,** that he should give eternal life to as many as thou hast given him.

   e) Romans 14:9
   > For to this end Christ both died, and rose, and revived, that he might be Lord both of the **dead and living.**

f) Ephesians 1:20-21
> Which he wrought in Christ, when he raised him from the dead, and set him at his own right hand in the heavenly places, Far above **all principality, and power, and might, and dominion, and every name that is named,** not only in this world, but also in that which is to come.

g) 1 Peter 3:22
> Who is gone into heaven, and is on the right hand of God; **angels and authorities and powers** being made subject unto him.

h) Revelation 17:14
> These shall make war with the Lamb, and the Lamb shall overcome them: for he is **Lord of lords, and King of kings:** and they that are with him are called, and chosen, and faithful.

The Authority of Jesus' Name

As believers in Jesus Christ, we have been given authority to use His name.

2. Use the following Scriptures to explain why the name of Jesus is important.

   a) Philippians 2:9-11
   > God has given Jesus a name that is above every other name. At the name of Jesus, every knee should bow in heaven, on earth, and under the earth; this implies that every living creature or created being must reverence the Lord Jesus Christ.

   b) John 20:31 and Acts 4:12
   > Salvation is available to us through the name of Jesus Christ our Lord. When we believe that Jesus is the Christ, the Son of God, we receive eternal life in His name.

   c) John 14:12-14
   > Believers can do the works that Jesus did and greater (more numerous) works because Jesus is with the Father. Jesus performs the requests that we ask of God in His name so that the Father can be glorified in the Son.

   d) John 15:5-8, 16
   > Without Jesus, we can do nothing. But He has chosen and

ordained us that we should go and bring forth fruit that remains. And whatever we ask the Father for (to fulfill our calling and do His will) in Jesus name, God will give it to us.
   e) Acts 10:43
      Through Jesus' name, our sins are forgiven.
   f) Ephesians 5:20 and Colossians 3:17
      We should give thanks to God in the name of our Lord Jesus Christ.

The Authority of New Testament Believers
The New Testament provides examples of early Christians who exercised spiritual authority.

3. Read Luke 9:1-6. Use these verses to answer the following questions.
   a) Who was called? (v. 1)
      The twelve disciples were called.
   b) Why were they sent out? (v. 2)
      The disciples were being sent out by Jesus to preach the kingdom of God and to heal the sick.
   c) Why did they need faith to go? (v. 3)
      They were instructed not to make natural preparations but to rely on God as they went.
   d) What did they do? (v. 6)
      They left and preached the Gospel and healed the sick everywhere.

4. Read Mark 16:14-20. Use these verses to answer the following questions.
   a) To whom did Jesus appear? (v. 14)
      Jesus appeared to the eleven disciples.
   b) What did He say to them? (v. 15)
      Jesus told them to go into all the world and preach the Gospel.
   c) By what authority will believers cast out devils? (v. 17)
      Believers will cast out devils by the authority in Jesus' name.
   d) Who was working with believers and confirming the Word with signs following? (v. 20)
      The Lord was working with believers and confirming the Word with signs following.

5. Read Acts 3:1-15. Use these verses to answer the following questions.
   a) Who was going into the temple? (v. 1)
      Peter and John.
   b) Who did they see? (v. 2)
      A man, who was born lame, lying at the temple gate.
   c) What did the man ask them? (v. 3)
      He asked for money.
   d) How did Peter respond? (vv. 4-6)
      Peter looked at him intently and commanded that the man look at them. Then Peter said, "Silver and gold have I none; but such as I have I give thee: In the name of Jesus Christ of Nazareth rise up and walk."
   e) What was it that Peter did not have? (v. 6a)
      Peter was not carrying money.
   f) What did Peter have? (v. 6b)
      Peter had the authority to heal the sick in the name of Jesus.
   g) What did Peter do? (v. 7)
      He took the man by the hand and lifted him up, and he was immediately healed.
   h) What did the man do? (v. 8)
      He entered the temple walking and leaping and praising God.
   i) When the people wondered about the man's healing, how did Peter respond? (vv. 12-15; see also Acts 4:10)
      Peter told them that it was not their power or holiness that healed the man. Then, he preached the Gospel and ended by saying that it was the power of the name of Jesus and the man's faith that had made him well.
   j) By what authority did Peter heal the sick?
      Peter healed the sick in the name of Jesus Christ.

6. Read Acts 16:16-18. Use these verses to answer the following questions.
   a) As Paul and other believers went to prayer, who did they encounter? (v. 16)
      A woman who was possessed by a spirit of divination.
   b) What did she do? (v. 17)
      She followed them for several days announcing to

everyone who they were.
  c) How did Paul respond? (v. 18a)
    After she did this for many days, Paul turned and command the spirit in her to come out in the name of Jesus Christ.
  d) What happened? (v. 18b)
    The spirit came out of her that same hour.
  e) By what authority did Paul cast out demons? (v. 18)
    Paul cast out demons in the name of Jesus Christ.

Our Authority in Jesus Christ
As believers in Christ, we have been given spiritual authority. Our confidence is not in ourselves but in the name of the Lord Jesus Christ whom we serve and in the truth of the Word of God.

7. Use the following verses to examine what God promises as we go forth in His name.
  a) Luke 10:19
    Jesus gives us power over the enemy
  b) John 10:28
    Through Jesus, we have eternal life. We shall never perish and no one can take us out of His hand.
  c) John 14:27
    Jesus gives us His peace. Therefore, we do not have to become troubled or afraid.
  d) 1 Corinthians 3:9
    We are laborers together with God.
  e) 1 Corinthians 15:57-58
    God gives us victory through our Lord Jesus Christ, and our labor is not in vain in the Lord.
  f) Hebrews 6:10
    God will remember our labor.
  g) Romans 8:33-39
    Christ Himself intercedes for us, and nothing shall separate us from His love. Through our Lord and Saviour Jesus Christ, we are more than conquerors.

LIFE APPLICATION

Personal Application
1. In the Bible, a person's name often carried the meaning of his or her entire character. In your own words, explain what Jesus meant when He said "in My name."

2. How should our spiritual authority over sin and Satan change the way we live in this world?

3. We are not only to speak peace, we are to be possessors of peace. Review your emotional responses. Where could you use Jesus' peace right now?
>   In a relationship?
>   In your work?
>   With some inner fear?
>   With a financial concern?

Examine your situation again in the light of Jesus' authority. Take hold of His peace and have faith in His ability and His promises to you today.

Church Ministry Application
1. Is the name of Jesus being exalted above every other name during the Sunday worship service?

2. Is our power and authority to use the name of Jesus being taught in Sunday School and Bible study classes?

3. When describing the harvest to His disciples, Jesus communicates a sense of urgency concerning evangelism. Today, we are closer to the coming of Jesus Christ than ever before. Is this same sense of urgency and need for committed laborers being communicated to the believers in your congregation?

SESSION SIX

JESUS WILL COME FOR YOU

For sessions of 90 minutes or more, use the lesson format for PART ONE and PART TWO.

PART ONE

ACTIVITY	TIME
Opening Prayer	5 minutes
Scripture Reading	5 minutes
Scripture Search	10 minutes
Chapter Highlights	20 minutes

PART TWO

ACTIVITY	TIME
Small Group Study	15 minutes
Large Group Presentations	25 minutes
Large Group Discussion	10 minutes
Closing Prayer	5 minutes

For sessions of less than 90 minutes, use PART ONE only and assign the Bible Study Application questions as homework.

Lesson Aims: At the end of this two-part Bible study session, the participants should be able to: a) summarize the predictions of the prophets, the teachings of Jesus, and the instructions of the angels and the apostles that relate to Jesus' return; b) recognize the signs of the end of the world and the return of the Lord; c) remember that God alone knows the time of Jesus' return; d) describe the proper attitudes and actions for believers who await the second coming of Jesus Christ.

PART ONE

A. OPENING PRAYER

Open the session with prayer. Include the requests that God would bless each participant to:

- Remember that Jesus Christ is coming back for His Church.
- Hold fast to sound doctrine and understand the signs of the times.
- Focus on the promise of Jesus' return instead of the timing.

- Live as those who are expectantly awaiting the return of the Lord

B. SCRIPTURE SEARCH
1. Ask someone to read 2 Peter 3:1-9 aloud to the group.

2. Ask for volunteers to answer the following questions:
    - Why were the two letters that make up the Epistles of 1 and 2 Peter written? (v. 1)
    - They were written as reminders to stimulate the believers to wholesome (pure) thinking. In other words, to encourage believers to hold on to the truths of God's Word.
    - What false doctrine or teaching does this passage of Scripture address?
    - 2 Peter 3:1-9 deals with the false teaching that Jesus will not return.
    - What were they instructed to recall? (v. 2)
    - They were instructed to recall the words of the prophets and the commands of the Lord Jesus given through the apostles.
    - What must they understand first of all? (v. 3)
    - The presence of scoffers is not unusual or unexpected. They must understand that in the last days scoffers will come.
    - Their behavior will include both scoffing and following their own evil desires.
    - What is a scoffer?
    - A person who expresses contempt verbally by laughter, mockery, ridicule, or sarcastic language.
    - What will these scoffers say? (v. 4)
    - They deny the truth of the second coming of the Jesus Christ. They ridicule Christ's promise to return, and justify their opinions by their own logic and reasoning. They say that since the early days of the faith "everything goes on as it has since the beginning of creation" (NIV). They argue that the natural world is not subject to divine intervention.
    - What truth do these scoffers deliberately forget? (vv. 5-7) Scoffers deliberately ignore the truth of God's Word. By His Word, God created the heavens and the earth. As a result of man's wickedness in the time of Noah, God destroyed the earth in the Flood. As God kept His first promise to destroy

the earth, He will also keep the second. According to His Word, the present heavens and earth are being kept for the day of judgment and the destruction of the ungodly by fire.
- What are the believers urged to remember? (v. 8)
- We must remember that God is not on our timetable or schedule. "With the Lord a day is like a thousand years and a thousand years are like a day" (NIV).
- Why has the Lord not yet fulfulled His promise to return? (v. 9)
- The Lord is not forgetful or slow concerning His promise. But He is patient and longsuffering with us, not wanting anyone to perish but everyone to come to repentance.

C. CHAPTER HIGHLIGHTS

Using the content of Chapter Six as background, give a general overview of the chapter. Be sure to include the following topics:
1. The Promised Return of Jesus Christ
2. The Words of the Prophets
3. The Account of the Gospels
4. The Teaching of the Apostles
5. The Problem with Focusing on the Time of Jesus' Return Instead of the Promise
6. The Believer's Response
   - Trust God's Word
   - Trust God's Timing

PART TWO

A. BIBLE STUDY APPLICATION
1. Introduction

The Bible Study Application section contains eight questions which provide an opportunity to examine our response to the return of Jesus Christ. The discussion of the Bible Study Application questions should confirm that the students understand that Jesus Christ is coming soon.

Allow as much time as necessary to encourage the exchange of ideas and insights. Use the information preceding each set of questions to help introduce or close the discussion of a topic. Use the Bible verses to help keep the discussion on track. Depending on the size and personality of the group, you can discuss as many or as few of the questions as needed.

2. Procedure
Select Small Group Leaders. Ask for volunteers or select five small group leaders. Then assign each small group leader a number from 1-5. (This can also be done beforehand to save time.) Ask the small group leaders to write their numbers on large sheets of white paper so that they can be seen from a distance.

Divide into Small Groups. Inform the participants that they will be separated into small groups. Each group will study a different set of questions and then will present their findings to the larger group at the end of the study period. The questions should be assigned as follows:

Group #1: The Return of Christ in the Words of Prophets (question 1)
Group #2: The Return of Christ in His Own Words (questions 2-3)
Group #3: The Return of Christ in the Words of the Angels and Apostles (question 4)
Group #4: The Timing of the Lord's Return (question 5)
Group #5: The Return of Christ and the Attitudes and Actions of Believers (questions 6-8)

Allow Participants to Count Off by Fives. Then ask them to follow the small group leader who is holding their assigned number. Identify the location of each group. (These locations can also be pre-printed on a sheet of paper, photocopied, and distributed to save time.) Participants should then assemble into smaller groups in their respective meeting areas.

Note: If the Bible Study is small, divide into three groups and eliminate discussion groups #1 and #3. You may want to include questions 1 and 5 as part of the homework assignment.

B. SMALL GROUP STUDY
1. Small Group Leaders
Each group will have one topic to explore. For each topic, there are questions and related Scripture references to stimulate discussion.

2. Sharing Insights
After 15 minutes, designate someone who will summarize the small group discussion within the larger body of participants. Remind the designated person that she or he will only have five minutes to present.

C. LARGE GROUP PRESENTATIONS

Reconvene the Group. Call the small groups back together.

Explain the Procedure. Explain that a representative of each small group will share that group's reflections on the Bible Study Application questions with the larger group.

Remind Small Group Representatives of the Time. Remind each group representative that he or she should try to summarize the group's discussion in less than five minutes. Allow up to five minutes to discuss each group's presentation.

D. LIFE APPLICATION DISCUSSION*

If time permits, the larger group can then discuss the Personal Application and Church Ministry questions together.

1. Introduction

The Personal Application section contains four questions which encourage the participants to consider the teaching in light of their own lives. The Church Ministry Application section contains three questions which address some implications for the congregation as a whole.

2. Sharing Insights

This discussion should be open-ended and voluntary. The sharing of personal insights or recommendations for church ministry should be encouraged but not required. The group may have quite a bit to say. Watch the clock! Stop them after 10 minutes.

*Answers are not provided for the Personal Application and Church Ministry sections because of the personal or specific nature of the questions.

E. PREPARATION FOR NEXT MEETING

Assignment. Have the participants read Chapter Seven, "On Being Loyal to Jesus as Lord" and review the questions in preparation for next week's session. Encourage them to come to the next session prepared to share their insights on the content of the chapter.

You may also want to assign small groups or particular questions to facilitate next week's meeting time.

Jesus Will Come For You **71**

F. CLOSING PRAYER
Hold hands, form a circle, and ask for specific prayer requests. Then ask for several volunteers to pray, keeping the prayer requests in mind.

ANSWERS TO BIBLE STUDY APPLICATION

The Return of Christ in the Words of the Prophets
1. Use the verses below to examine what the prophets foretold about the Day of the Lord.
   a) Isaiah 13:9-11
   - What did the Prophet Isaiah say about the Day of the Lord? Isaiah describes it as a cruel day of wrath and fierce anger when the land will be made desolate, sinners will be destroyed, and the sun, the stars, and the moon will no longer shine.
   - Who will be punished? The world will be punished for evil and sinners will be punished for their sin.

   b) Daniel 7:13-14
   - What did the Prophet Daniel say about the Day of the Lord? Daniel describes a day when the Son of man comes from heaven with the clouds and is given everlasting dominion and glory and a kingdom that cannot be destroyed. In God's kingdom, who will serve the Lord? (See also Hebrews 12:28.)
   - All nations, people, and those of every language shall serve the Lord in His kingdom.

   c) Joel 2:1-11, 31-32
   - What did the Prophet Joel say about the Day of the Lord? Joel describes a great and dreadful day of darkness, fire, earthquake, fierce battle, death, and destruction.
   - Who will be delivered or saved? (See also Acts 2:21.) Everyone who calls on the name of the Lord will be saved.

   d) Zephaniah 1:14-18
   - What did the Prophet Zephaniah say about the Day of the Lord?

Zephaniah describes a day of wrath, trouble, distress, darkness, and destruction.
- Why will distress and destruction come upon mankind?
Distress and destruction will come because they have sinned against the Lord.

e) Malachi 4:1-2
- What did the Prophet Malachi say about the Day of the Lord?
Malachi describes it as a day of destruction for the wicked and of healing and protection for the righteous.
- To whom is God's promise of salvation given? (See also Acts 13:26.)
God's promise is given to those who fear Him.

f) Jude 14-15
- What did Enoch, who lived seven generations after Adam, prophesy about the Day of the Lord?
Enoch describes a day when the Lord will come with ten thousand of His saints to execute judgement and convict the ungodly of their sins.
- Who will be with the Lord when He comes? (See also 1 Thessalonians 3:13.)
The saints of the Lord will come with Him.

The Return of Christ in His Own Words

2. Read Matthew 24:3-30. Use these verses to explore how Jesus described His second coming.
   a) Why should we pay attention to the signs of the times? (v. 4)
   Jesus tells us to take heed to the signs of His coming and of the end of the age so that we will not be deceived.

   b) List the earthly signs that indicate that Jesus' return and the end of the world is near.
   Verse 5: People who claim to be Christ will deceive many.
   Verse 6: Wars and rumors of wars will increase.
   Verse 7: Nation will rise against nation, and there will be disease and disaster, including famines, pestilences, and earthquakes in various places.

Verse 9:	Persecution will increase. The saints will suffer affliction, murder, and hatred because of the name of Jesus Christ.
Verse 10:	There will be contention and confusion. Many people will become offended, betray one another, and hate others.
Verse 11:	False prophets will arise who will deceive many.
Verses 12-13:	Because sin will abound, the love of many will grow cold but believers who endure to the end shall be saved.
Verse 14:	The Gospel will be preached in all the world as a witness to all nations.

    c) How will the distress and tribulation of this time compare to other times in history? (v. 21)
        The tribulation of this time will be greater than any other time in the past or future.

    d) How will the believers endure this time of tribulation? (v. 22)
        For the elect's sake, these days will be shortened.

    e) How will believers distinguish the appearance of false Christs from the Lord's return? (vv. 23-27)
        The Lord Jesus Christ is not a mere man; we will not have to go out to find Him. His return will be a supernatural event that all the world will see.

    f) What signs will appear in the heavens? (v. 29)
        The sun, moon, and stars will be darkened and the powers of the heavens will be shaken.

    g) After these signs occur in the heavens, what will happen? (v. 30)
        The Lord Jesus Christ will appear coming in the clouds of heaven in power and glory. The people on earth will mourn and everyone will see Him.

3. Read Matthew 25:31-34, 41, 46. Use these verses to discuss what Jesus will do when He returns.
    a) When Jesus comes in His glory, who will He separate? (v. 32)
        He will separate the people of the nations, believers from

unbelievers, as a shepherd separates his sheep from the goats.

b) What will Jesus say to believers? (v. 34)
"Come, ye blessed of my Father, inherit the kingdom prepared for you from the foundation of the world."

c) What will Jesus say to unbelievers? (v. 41)
"Depart from me, ye cursed, into everlasting fire, prepared for the devil and his angels."

d) What will happen to the unbelievers? (v. 46)
They shall go away to everlasting punishment.

e) What will happen to the believers? (v. 46)
They shall go into eternal life.

The Return of Christ in the Words of the Angels and Apostles

4. Fill in the blanks below to examine what the angels and apostles taught believers about the return of the Lord Jesus Christ.

   a) Acts 1:9-11

   And when he had spoken these things, while they beheld, he was taken up; and a cloud received him out of their sight. And while they looked stedfastly toward heaven as he went up, behold, two men stood by them in white apparel; Which also said, Ye men of Galilee, why stand ye gazing up into heaven? this same Jesus, which is taken up from you into heaven, shall so come in **like manner as ye have seen him go into heaven.**

   b) Colossians 3:4

   When Christ, who is our life, shall appear, then shall ye also **appear with him in glory.**

   c) 1 Thessalonians 4:16-17

   For the Lord himself shall descend from heaven with a shout, with the voice of the archangel, and with the trump of God: and the dead in Christ **shall rise first:** Then we which are alive and remain shall be **caught up together with them in the clouds, to meet the Lord in the air:** and so shall we ever be with the Lord.

   d) 2 Timothy 4:8

Henceforth there is laid up for me a crown of righteousness, which the Lord, the righteous judge, shall give me at that day: and not to me only, but unto **all them also that love his appearing.**

e) 1 Peter 5:4

And when the chief Shepherd shall appear, ye shall receive **a crown of glory** that fadeth not away.

f) 1 John 3:2

Beloved, now are we the sons of God, and it doth not yet appear what we shall be: but we know that, when he shall appear, **we shall be like him;** for we shall see him as he is.

g) Revelation 1:7

Behold, **he cometh with clouds;** and every eye shall see him, and they also which pierced him: and all kindreds of the earth shall wail because of him. Even so, Amen.

The Timing of the Lord's Return

5. Match the following verses with their description to review what God's Word says about the timing of the Lord's return.

a. Matthew 24:26 and Mark 13:32-33

b. Matthew 24:27 and Mark 13:36

c. Matthew 24:44 and Luke 12:40

d. 1 Thessalonians 5:2 and Revelation 3:3

e. Hebrews 10:37

f. Revelation 3:11 and 22:7, 20

d Silently, without warning

b Suddenly, for all to see

e Soon, without delay

a Surprisingly, at a time unknown to mankind

f Quickly, in God's divine time-frame

c Unexpectedly, when people think not

The Return of Christ and the Attitudes and Actions of Believers

6. Match the verses below with the proper attitudes for believers who await the return of the Lord.

a. Luke 12:40 — a Readiness
b. Luke 19:13 — c Patient Waiting
c. 1 Corinthians 1:7 and James 5:8 — h Watchfulness
d. 1 Corinthians 1:8 and 1 Thessalonians 5:23 — g Abiding
e. 1 Timothy 6:14 — e Obedience
f. Titus 2:13 — f Expectation
g. 1 John 2:28 — d Blameless Living
h. Revelation 16:15 and Luke 12:37 — b Faithful Stewardship

7. Use the following verses to discuss why those who believe in Jesus Christ can confidently look forward to the coming of the Day of the Lord.
    a) John 3:36 and 1 John 2:17
        Whoever believes in Jesus Christ has everlasting life.
    b) Philippians 1:6
        We can be confident that God who began a good work in us will continue to perform it until the return of our Lord Jesus Christ.
    c) Jude 23-24
        Our God is able to keep us from falling and to present us into His glorious presence without fault and with great joy.
    d) 1 John 2:28
        We know that if we abide in Him, we may have confidence and we will not be ashamed at His coming.

8. Use the following verses to determine how the coming of the Lord should affect the actions of the believer.
    a) According to Matthew 6:10, how should the return of Christ affect our **prayer?**
        We should pray for God's kingdom to come.
    b) According to Matthew 24:14, how should the return of Christ affect our **witnessing?**
        We should witness and preach the Gospel to everyone.
    c) According to 2 Peter 3:11-12, how should the return of Christ affect our **conduct?**

> We should endeavor to be holy in conversation and conduct.
>
> d) Read 2 Corinthians 11:2; Ephesians 5:27; and James 1:27. According to these verses, how should the return of Christ affect our **purity**?
>
> > We should abstain from sin, avoid worldliness, and pursue holiness.
>
> e) According to 1 John 2:15-17, how should the return of Christ affect our **affections**?
>
> > We should not love the world or the things of the world.
>
> f) According to John 9:4 and Colossians 4:5-7, how should the return of Christ affect our **Christian service**?
>
> > We should be busy doing God's work and His will before Jesus returns.

LIFE APPLICATION

Personal Application

1. Dig deep, use your imagination, and take time to really consider and write down your answers to the following hypothetical questions:
   - If Jesus came today would you be sad or glad? Why?
   - If you were in charge of the world's clock would you slow it down or speed it up? Why?
   - If you were in charge of creating, redeeming, and destroying the world which would you take more "time" doing? Why?

2. When we remind ourselves that nothing on earth is permanent, we will be reassured by the fact that Jesus' kingdom is not an earthly kingdom.
   - How should this truth change the way that you live?
   - Do you sometimes live as though this life is all there is?
   - Are you able to let go of the things of this life?
   - Review the proper attitudes for believers listed in question 6.
   - Identify one or two attitudes that you can develop this week. Look up the related Scriptures. Ask God to help you look forward in faith to Christ's return.

3. The Lord Jesus Christ shall surely return and bring about justice. In general, if Christ were to return today, what degree of faith would He find in your heart? Use the scale below, where 10 represents strong, unwavering faith, to record your honest personal evaluation.

1 2 3 4 5 6 7 8 9 10

Remember that "faith comes by hearing, and hearing by the word of God" (Romans 10:17).

4. Now answer the following specific questions:
- Read the parable of the ten virgins in Matthew 25:1-13.
- How should you prepare for the coming of Jesus Christ?
- Read the parable of the traveling man and his servants in Matthew 25:14-30. Over what has God given you stewardship? How can you become a more profitable servant of Christ before the Lord returns?
- Read Jesus' description of His second coming and His view of good works from Matthew 25:31-46. How would you explain the end times and the Day of the Lord to a seeker or new believer?

Church Ministry Application
1. "Let us know, let us press on to know the Lord; his going forth is sure as the dawn; he will come to us as the showers, as the spring rains that water the earth" (Hosea 6:3, RSV). If we are to walk in step with the Master, we must be ready. How can the members of the congregation be encouraged to prepare for the Day of the Lord?

2. How often are the members challenged to evaluate their lives in light of the coming of Jesus Christ? As the Day of the Lord approaches, is the truth of the second coming of Christ used to stimulate witnessing for Christ and Christian service?

3. In the last days, false teachers, false prophets, and false Christs will appear.
   Like Peter, are your church leaders and teachers stirring up believers to wholesome (pure) thinking?
   Are the members of the congregation being taught to know and heed the signs of the times?
   Are they being equipped with the knowledge of God's Word so that they will be able to hold fast to sound doctrine and discern truth from error?

SESSION SEVEN
ON BEING LOYAL TO JESUS AS LORD

For sessions of 90 minutes or more, use the lesson format for PART ONE and PART TWO.

PART ONE

ACTIVITY	TIME
Opening Prayer	5 minutes
Scripture Reading	5 minutes
Scripture Search	10 minutes
Chapter Highlights	20 minutes

PART TWO

ACTIVITY	TIME
Small Group Study	15 minutes
Large Group Presentations	25 minutes
Large Group Discussion	10 minutes
Closing Prayer	5 minutes

For sessions of less than 90 minutes, use PART ONE only and assign the Bible Study Application questions as homework.

Lesson Aims: At the end of this two-part Bible study session, the participants should: a) know how to declare and demonstrate their love and loyalty to Jesus Christ; b) understand that their commitment to Christ will be tested; c) remember that the Lord will renew and restore us when our loyalty fails.

PART ONE

A. OPENING PRAYER

Open the session with prayer. Include the requests that God would bless each participant to:

- Reaffirm or commit their loyalty to Jesus Christ as Lord.
- Stand for Christ in times of temptation, trial, or testing.
- Remember that God is ready to forgive and restore us whenever we fail.

B. SCRIPTURE SEARCH

1. Ask someone to read John 13:33, 36-38 aloud to the group.

2. Ask for volunteers to answer the following questions:
    - In this passage of Scripture, where is Jesus about to go?
      Jesus is going to die on the cross.
    - How would you describe Peter's positive qualities in this passage?
      Answers will vary. Some positive qualities may include: inquisitive, full of zeal, determined, possessing good intentions, persistant, self-confident, etc..
    - How would you describe Peter's negative qualities in this passage?
      Answers will vary. Some negative qualities may include: misguided, impulsive, failing to understand the words of Jesus, focused on his own assumptions, refusing to take "no" for an answer, etc..
    - What does Peter declare in verse 37?
      Peter declares that he will lay down his life for Jesus.
    - How does Jesus respond to Peter's declaration in verse 38?
      Jesus questions Peter's willingness to die for Him and tells Peter that he will deny Him three times before the cock crows tomorrow morning.

3. Ask someone to read John 18:15-18, 25-27 aloud to the group.

4. Ask for volunteers to answer the following questions:
    - After Jesus' arrest, why was Peter waiting outside the door of the high priest's courtyard? (v. 15)
      Peter was following Jesus.
    - Why does Peter deny being a disciple of Jesus?
      Peter is beginning to understand the seriousness of Jesus' arrest and his own potential danger. Peter's resolve to give his life for Jesus dissappears, and he denies any association with Him in order to protect himself.
    - How do you think Peter felt when he heard the cock crow?
      Answers will vary. (See Mark 14:72 and Luke 22:62.)

5. Ask someone to read John 21:15-25 aloud to the group.

6. Ask for volunteers to answer the following questions:
    - When Jesus Christ appears to the disciples, what question

On Being Loyal to Jesus as Lord **81**

 does He ask Peter?
- Jesus asks Peter if he loves Him. ("Loveth thou me . . . ?") How many times does Jesus question Peter's love for Him?
- Jesus questions Peter's love for Him three times. Each time that Peter affirms his love, Jesus tells him to do something. How is Peter supposed to demonstrate his love and loyalty to Jesus now?
- Jesus commands Peter to care for the believers by telling him to "Feed my lambs," (v. 15) and "Feed my sheep" (vv. 16-17).
- Jesus foretold Peter's denial in John 13:38. What prophecy does Jesus give about Peter in John 21:18-19?
  Jesus describes the manner of death Peter would suffer to glorify God.
- What does Jesus' new prediction indicate about Peter?
- Jesus' prediction indicates that Peter will fulfill his declaration of love and loyalty to the Lord. Peter's death will glorify God.
- After He describes Peter's death, what does Jesus tell Peter to do in verse 19?
  Jesus tells Peter to follow Him.
- How do you think Peter felt when he heard Jesus say "follow me"?
  Answers will vary.

7. Summarize the events from John 13:33, 36-38; 18:15-18, 25-27; and 21:15-25 as follows:
   - In the Upper Room, Peter declares his love for and loyalty to Jesus.
   - After Jesus was arrested, Peter's declaration was tested on three occasions by different accusers.
   - By denying that he knew Jesus, Peter proved that in spite of his prior, sincere declaration he was not yet willing to die for Jesus. Although Peter had declared his love and loyalty to Jesus, he was not ready to demonstrate it.
   - Point out, however, that Peter continued to follow Jesus.
   - Some Bible scholars say that Jesus asked Peter to declare His love three times in order to cancel out His three-fold denial.

- By charging Peter three times to care for believers, Jesus restores Peter to his former position as leader.
- Finally, Jesus gives Peter the same invitation and instruction that He gave before His death and resurrection: "Follow me."
- Note that Peter follows and asks questions.

8. Conclude the discussion by explaining that:
    - Jesus said, "Greater love hath no man than this, that a man lay down his life for his friends" (John 15:13).
    - By declaring that he would lay down his life for Jesus, Peter was making the ultimate declaration of love for and loyalty to Jesus.
    - Point out that a **declaration** of love and loyalty is a good beginning, but the truth becomes evident by our **demonstration.**
    - Jesus Christ made the ultimate declaration of love for us. He said, "I am the good shepherd: the good shepherd giveth his life for the sheep" (John 10:11).
    - We know from the account in the garden of Gethsemane that the prospect of death on the cross, being cut off from the Father, and the terrible burden of bearing the world's sins appalled Jesus (Matthew 26:36-46). Yet He demonstrated His love by enduring the cross because of what it would achieve. Jesus willingly gave His life for us.
    - When conversing with Peter after His resurrection, Jesus refers to believers as lambs and sheep. Jesus may have been reminding Peter that He fulfilled His declaration of love for us. Jesus declared and demonstrated that He is the Good Shepherd who gave His life for the sheep.

C. CHAPTER HIGHLIGHTS

Using the content of Chapter Seven as background, give a general overview of the chapter. Be sure to include the following topics:
1. The Meaning of Loyalty
2. Declared Loyalty to Jesus is Just the Beginning
3. Loyalty Comes through Knowledge of Jesus
4. Why Should We Be Loyal to Jesus?
5. Loyalty Will Be Tested

6. When Your Loyalty Fails
7. Renewal of Loyalty Is Possible

PART TWO
A. BIBLE STUDY APPLICATION
1. Introduction

The Bible Study Application section contains six questions which provide an opportunity to examine our loyalty to the Lordship of Jesus Christ. The discussion of the Bible Study Application questions should confirm that the students understand that believers must declare and demonstrate their love for Christ.

Allow as much time as necessary to encourage the exchange of ideas and insights. Use the information preceding each set of questions to help introduce or close the discussion of a topic. Use the Bible verses to help keep the discussion on track. Depending on the size and personality of the group, you can discuss as many or as few of the questions as needed.

2. Procedure

Select Small Group Leaders. Ask for volunteers or select four small group leaders. Then assign each small group leader a number from 1-4. (This can also be done beforehand to save time.) Ask the small group leaders to write their numbers on large sheets of white paper so that they can be seen from a distance.

Divide into Small Groups. Inform the participants that they will be separated into small groups. Each group will study a different set of questions and then will present their findings to the larger group at the end of the study period. The questions should be assigned as follows:

Group #1: Declared Loyalty Is the Beginning
(questions 1-2)
Group #2: Demonstrating Our Declaration (question 3)
Group #3: Jesus Is Asking: "Do You Love Me?"
(questions 4-5)
Group #4: When Our Loyalty Fails, Renewal Is Possible
(question 6)

Allow Participants to Count Off by Fours. Then ask them to follow the small group leader who is holding their assigned number. Identify the location of each group. (These locations can also be pre-printed on a sheet of paper, photocopied, and distributed to save time.) Participants should then assemble into smaller groups in their respective meeting areas.

B. SMALL GROUP STUDY

1. **Small Group Leaders**
   Each group will have one topic to explore. For each topic, there are questions and related Scripture references to stimulate discussion.

2. **Sharing Insights**
   After 15 minutes, designate someone who will summarize the small group discussion within the larger body of participants. Remind the designated person that she or he will only have five minutes to present.

C. LARGE GROUP PRESENTATIONS

Reconvene the Group. Call the small groups back together.

Explain the Procedure. Explain that a representative of each small group will share that group's reflections on the Bible Study Application questions with the larger group.

Remind Small Group Representatives of the Time. Remind each group representative that he or she should try to summarize the group's discussion in less than five minutes. Allow up to five minutes to discuss each group's presentation.

D. LIFE APPLICATION DISCUSSION*

If time permits, the larger group can then discuss the Personal Application and Church Ministry questions together.

1. **Introduction**
   The Personal Application section contains four questions which encourage the participants to consider the teaching in light of their own lives. The Church Ministry Application section contains three questions which address some implications for the congregation as a whole.

2. **Sharing Insights**
   This discussion should be open-ended and voluntary. The sharing of personal insights or recommendations for church ministry should be encouraged but not required. The group may have quite a bit to say. Watch

the clock! Stop them after 10 minutes.

*Answers are not provided for the Personal Application and Church Ministry sections because of the personal or specific nature of the questions.

E. PREPARATION FOR NEXT MEETING

Assignment. Have the participants read Chapter Eight, "You Can Believe" and review the questions in preparation for next week's session. Encourage them to come to the next session prepared to share their insights on the content of the chapter.

You may also want to assign small groups or particular questions to facilitate next week's meeting time.

F. CLOSING PRAYER

Hold hands, form a circle, and ask for specific prayer requests. Then ask for several volunteers to pray, keeping the prayer requests in mind.

ANSWERS TO BIBLE STUDY APPLICATION

Declared Loyalty Is the Beginning

Our declaration of love and loyalty to Jesus Christ reveals our commitment, clarifies our intentions, establishes our priorities, and anchors our purpose in life.

1. Use the following verses to review some of the declarations of loyalty that are recorded in the Bible.
    a) Joshua 24:15
        - Who is speaking to whom?
        - Joshua is speaking to the people of Israel.
        - What instruction does he give to them?
        - He tells the people to choose whom they will serve.
        - What does he declare?
        - Joshua declares, ". . . but as for me and my house, we will serve the Lord."

    b) Ruth 1:16
        - Who is speaking to whom?
        - Ruth is speaking to Naomi.
        - What does she ask her not to do?
        - Ruth asks Naomi not to tell her to leave or to go back from following her.

- What does she declare?
- Ruth declares her loyalty to Naomi by stating, ". . . for whither thou goest, I will go; and where thou lodgest, I will lodge: thy people shall be my people, and thy God my God."

c) 1 Kings 18:21, 24
- Who is speaking to whom?
- Elijah is speaking to the people of Israel.
- What does he challenge them to do?
- He challenges the people to choose whom they will follow.
- What does he declare?
- Elijah declares, "I will call on the name of the Lord: and the God that answereth by fire, let him be God."

d) Psalm 119:115
- Who is speaking to whom?
- David is speaking to those who do evil.
- What does he declare?
- David declares, "I will keep the commandments of my God."

e) Isaiah 50:7
- Who is speaking?
  Isaiah is speaking.
- What does he declare?
  Isaiah declares, ". . . therefore have I set my face like a flint, and I know that I shall not be ashamed."

f) Acts 21:13
- Who is speaking?
  Paul is speaking.
- What does he declare?
  Paul declares, ". . . I am ready not to be bound only, but also to die at Jerusalem for the name of the Lord Jesus."

2. Fill in the blanks in the verses below to review the value of confessing Jesus Christ as Lord.
   a) Matthew 10:32
   Whosoever therefore shall confess me before men, **him will I confess also before my Father; which is in heaven.**

b) Romans 10:9
> That if thou shalt confess with thy mouth the Lord Jesus, and shalt believe in thine heart that God hath raised him from the dead, **thou shalt be saved.**

c) Philippians 2:11
> And that every tongue should confess that Jesus Christ is Lord, **to the glory of God the Father.**

d) 1 John 4:15
> Whosoever shall confess that Jesus is the Son of God, **God dwelleth in him, and he in God.**

Demonstrating Our Declaration of Loyalty

Although our declaration of faith, love, and loyalty to Christ is important, it is only the beginning. Lip-service and good intentions alone are not enough. We must also demonstrate true commitment to our Lord and Saviour Jesus Christ.

3. Use the following verses to determine why our declaration alone is not enough.
   a) Ezekiel 33:31
      - What four things were the people doing right?
        The people came to worship God, they sat before the Lord, they heard the Word, and they declared their love for God.
      - What two things were they doing wrong?
        Although they came to church, heard the sermon, and said all the right things, they did not obey God's Word and they desired the things of life more than they desired the plan and approval of God.
      - In addition to declaring our love and loyalty, what two things does this verse imply we must do? (See also 1 Samuel 15:22 and Matthew 6:33.)
        We must obey God fully, and seek Him first.

   b) Isaiah 29:13 and Matthew 15:7-9
      - What two things were the people doing right?
        The people drew near to God with their mouth (called upon the name of the Lord), and they honored (praised) God with their lips.
      - What two things were they doing wrong?

Although they praised God and called on His name, in reality their hearts were far from God, and their religious worship was based on the commandments and traditions of men.
- In addition to declaring our love and loyalty, what two things do these verses imply we must do? (See also James 4:8 and John 4:23-24.)
  We must have a heart that draws near to the Lord and shuns sin, and we must worship God sincerely according to His Word.
- In Matthew 15:7, Jesus uses the term "hypocrites." What is a hypocrite?
  A hypocrite is a pretender; a person who conceals their true nature, motives, or feelings behind a false appearance; someone who says one thing and does another.
- Although the people said the right things, what does Matthew 15:9 say about their worship?
  They worshiped God in vain.

c) Matthew 7:21 and Luke 6:46
- What were the people rightly calling Jesus?
  The people were calling Jesus Lord.
- What were they doing wrong?
  They did not obey Jesus.
- In addition to declaring our love and loyalty, what else must we do?
  We must obey the Word of our Lord and Saviour Jesus Christ.
- When we declare that Jesus is our Lord, what does it mean?
  We are declaring that we belong to Jesus. We are saying that He is our Master and we are His servants. We are giving Jesus the right to govern and control our lives, and we are proclaiming that we will honor, obey, and serve Him.

Jesus Is Asking: "Do You Love Me?"
Like Peter, we each must answer the question of whether we love Jesus. We answer this question not only with our words, but also by actions which demonstrate our love for Jesus Christ.

4. Complete the following verses from the Gospel of John to examine what Jesus says about those who love Him.
   a) John 14:15
   > If ye love me, **keep my commandments.**
   b) John 14:21
   > He that **hath my commandments, and keepeth them,** he it is that loveth me: and he that loveth me shall be loved of my Father, and I will love him, and will manifest myself to him.
   c) John 14:23
   > Jesus answered and said unto him, If a man love me, he will **keep my words:** and my Father will love him, and we will come unto him, and make our abode with him.

5. Complete the following verses from John's epistles to discover how to demonstrate our love for the Lord.
   a) 1 John 2:5-6
   > But whoso **keepeth his word,** in him verily is the love of God perfected: hereby know we that we are in him. He that saith he abideth in him ought himself also so to **walk, even as he walked.**
   b) 1 John 2:15-17
   > Love not the world, neither the things that are in the world. If any man love the world, the love of the Father is not in him. For all that is in the world, the lust of the flesh, and the lust of the eyes, and the pride of life, is not of the Father, but is of the world. And the world passeth away, and the lust thereof: but he that **doeth the will of God** abideth for ever.
   c) 1 John 3:18
   > My little children, let us not love in word, neither in tongue; but in **deed and in truth.**
   d) 1 John 4:20
   > If a man say, I love God, and **hateth his brother,** he is a liar: for he that loveth not **his brother whom he hath seen,** how can he love God whom he hath not seen?
   e) 1 John 5:3
   > For this is the love of God, that we **keep his commandments:** and his commandments are not grievous.
   f) 2 John 1:6

And this is love, that we **walk after his commandments.** This is the commandment, That, as ye have heard from the beginning, ye should walk in it.

When Our Loyalty Fails, Renewal Is Possible
Jesus Christ is the same yesterday, today, and forever (Hebrews 13:8). Whenever we return to the Lord, He will restore our faith, hope, love, and commitment.

6. Use the following verses to discover what we should do when we commit sin or experience failure.
    a) 1 John 1:9
        - What should we do when we have sinned?
          We should confess our sins to God.
        - What does God promise to do?
          God will forgive us and cleanse us from unrighteousness.

    b) Isaiah 55:7
        - What should we do when we have sinned?
          We should forsake our wicked ways and our unrighteous thoughts, and return to God.
        - What does God promise to do?
          God will have mercy on us and abundantly pardon us.

    c) Jeremiah 3:22
        - What should we do when we have fallen away from God?
          We should return to God.
        - What does God promise to do?
          God will heal our backsliding.

    d) Hosea 14:1-2, 4
        - What should we do when we have fallen into sin?
          We should return to the Lord in prayer and humbly ask Him to take away our sins and receive us because of His grace.
        - What does God promise when we do this?
          God will heal our backsliding, love us freely, and turn His anger from us.

    e) Malachi 3:7
        - What should we do when we have broken God's law?

We should return to God.
- What does God promise to do?
  God will return to us.

f) Matthew 6:14
- What else must we do to receive forgiveness?
  We must forgive others.
- When we do that, what will God do?
  When we forgive others, God will forgive us.

g) Hebrews 8:10, 12
- What has God promised to do for His people?
  God will be merciful and forgive our sins.

h) Proverbs 28:13
- When we cover our sins, what will happen?
  We will not prosper.
- When we confess and forsake sin, what will we receive?
  When we confess and forsake sin, we will receive mercy.

LIFE APPLICATION

Personal Application

1. Why is it easy to declare your love and loyalty to Jesus when you have an "Upper Room" experience? Why should we expect that our declaration of loyalty and commitment to Jesus Christ will be tested?

2. Have you ever come close to blowing it so badly that you thought that God wouldn't or couldn't forgive you? What did you discover about God through this experience?

3. Write down your own definition of loyalty.

4. With this definition in mind, answer the following general questions:
    - How is God loyal to us?
    - Why is God loyal to us?
    - What are the benefits of professing our loyalty to Christ?

Then answer the following personal questions:
    - How can you demonstrate your loyalty to Christ?
    - In light of your commitment to Christ, how should you demonstrate your loyalty to others?

Church Ministry Application
1. Today, the word "loyalty" is seldom used. How can the value of loyalty be emphasized and taught to the children, youth, and adults in the congregation?

2. Believers should not be surprised when they face misunderstanding, challenges, or even outright opposition because of their faith in Jesus Christ. How can the congregation become better equipped to stand for Christ during times of testing?

3. God forgives those who turn to Him, repent, confess, and forsake sin. How can the church become more effective as a place of renewal and restoration for believers who have failed but now desire to return to the Lord?

SESSION EIGHT

YOU CAN BELIEVE

For sessions of 90 minutes or more, use the lesson format for PART ONE and PART TWO.

PART ONE

ACTIVITY	TIME
Opening Prayer	5 minutes
Scripture Reading	5 minutes
Scripture Search	10 minutes
Chapter Highlights	20 minutes

PART TWO

ACTIVITY	TIME
Small Group Study	15 minutes
Large Group Presentations	25 minutes
Large Group Discussion	10 minutes
Closing Prayer	5 minutes

For sessions of less than 90 minutes, use PART ONE only and assign the Bible Study Application questions as homework.

Lesson Aims: At the end of this two-part Bible study session, the participants should be able to: a) explain the importance of faith; b) recognize the basic beliefs of Christianity; c) evaluate their faith in Jesus Christ; d) know how to respond when faced with doubts about who Jesus is or questions about God.

PART ONE

A. OPENING PRAYER

Open the session with prayer. Include the requests that God would bless each participant to:
- Believe the Word of God.
- Believe in Jesus Christ the Lord.

B. SCRIPTURE SEARCH

1. Invite the class to close their eyes as they listen to the following fictionalized report.
   Imagine you are there:
   - You thought He was the Messiah.
   - You left everything to follow Him.

- He had wisdom and power above and beyond anything you'd ever known.
- But now He was dead.
- Not killed as He valiantly fought for freedom.
- But crucified in pain and shame between two criminals.
- You always felt that something bad was going to happen, but nothing like this.
- He's dead, and it's over.
- But the others just can't seem to accept it. They don't know when to give up.
- They *even* say they've seen Him.
- How could anyone blame you if you ask for proof?
- How can you believe again?
- You challenge them to show you.

2. Ask someone to read John 20:24-29 aloud to the group.

3. Ask for volunteers to answer the following questions:
    - What evidence did Thomas require before he would believe the disciple's report of Jesus' resurrection?

      Thomas would not believe until he saw and touched the print of the nails in Jesus' hands, and put his hand into the wound in His side.

    - If Thomas did not receive tangible proof, what had he determined to do?

      Thomas had determined that if he did not see Jesus for himself, he would not believe.

    - In light of the information given in verse 26, how do you think Jesus entered the room?

      Answers will vary. Jesus entered supernaturally. He may have simply appeared in their midst; or He could have come into their midst by walking through an unopened door or solid wall.

    - How does Jesus greet the disciples when He appears? Jesus says, "Peace be unto you."

- What does Jesus say to Thomas?

    Jesus responds Thomas' need to see and feel for himself. He satisfies Thomas' demand for proof by inviting Him to look at and touch His wounds.

- What does Jesus challenge Thomas to do?

    Jesus tells Thomas to "be not faithless, but believing."

- After Jesus presents Thomas with the evidence of His resurrected body and challenges him to believe, how does Thomas respond?

    Thomas says, "My Lord and my God."

- What did Thomas' answer indicate?

    Thomas' answer indicates that he now believes that Jesus is Lord and God.

- Who are those whom Jesus says are blessed?

    We are blessed who have not seen Jesus, yet have believed in Him.

C. CHAPTER HIGHLIGHTS

Using the content of Chapter Eight as background, give a general overview of the chapter. Be sure to include the following topics:
1. Skepticism Exposed
2. Encountering the Master
3. Belief Rekindled
4. The Blessing of Believing

PART TWO

A. BIBLE STUDY APPLICATION
1. Introduction

    The Bible Study Application section contains eight questions which provide an opportunity to examine the importance of believing that Jesus Christ is Lord and putting our faith in Him. The discussion of the Bible Study Application questions should confirm that the students understand that in every situation we can believe God's promises.

Allow as much time as necessary to encourage the exchange of ideas and insights. Use the information preceding each set of questions to help introduce or close the discussion of a topic. Use the Bible verses to help keep the discussion on track. Depending on the size and personality of the group, you can discuss as many or as few of the questions as needed.

2. **Procedure**

Select Small Group Leaders. Ask for volunteers or select four small group leaders. Then assign each small group leader a number from 1-4. (This can also be done beforehand to save time.) Ask the small group leaders to write their numbers on large sheets of white paper so that they can be seen from a distance.

Divide into Small Groups. Inform the participants that they will be separated into small groups. Each group will study a different set of questions and then will present their findings to the larger group at the end of the study period. The questions should be assigned as follows:

Group #1: What Does It Mean to Believe? (questions 1-2)
Group #2: We Believe that the Bible is the Inspired Word of God (questions 3-4)
Group #3: We Believe in the Deity of Jesus Christ (questions 5-7)
Group #4: We Believe and Rely on the Finished Work of Jesus Christ (question 8)

Allow Participants to Count Off by Fours. Then ask them to follow the small group leader who is holding their assigned number. Identify the location of each group. (These locations can also be pre-printed on a sheet of paper, photocopied, and distributed to save time.) Participants should then assemble into smaller groups in their respective meeting areas.

Note: If the Bible Study is small, divide into three groups and eliminate discussion group #2. You may want to include questions 3-4 as part of the homework assignment.

B. SMALL GROUP STUDY

1. **Small Group Leaders**

Each group will have one topic to explore. For each topic, there are questions and related Scripture references to stimulate discussion.

2. **Sharing Insights**

After 15 minutes, designate someone who will summarize the small group discussion within the larger body of participants. Remind the designated person that she or he will only have five minutes to present.

C. LARGE GROUP PRESENTATIONS

Reconvene the Group. Call the small groups back together.

Explain the Procedure. Explain that a representative of each small group will share that group's reflections on the Bible Study Application questions with the larger group.

Remind Small Group Representatives of the Time. Remind each group representative that he or she should try to summarize the group's discussion in less than five minutes. Allow up to five minutes to discuss each group's presentation.

D. LIFE APPLICATION DISCUSSION*

If time permits, the larger group can then discuss the Personal Application and Church Ministry questions together.

1. Introduction

The Personal Application section contains five questions which encourage the participants to consider the teaching in light of their own lives. The Church Ministry Application section contains three questions which address some implications for the congregation as a whole.

2. Sharing Insights

This discussion should be open-ended and voluntary. The sharing of personal insights or recommendations for church ministry should be encouraged but not required. The group may have quite a bit to say. Watch the clock! Stop them after 10 minutes.

*Answers are not provided for the Personal Application and Church Ministry sections because of the personal or specific nature of the questions.

E. PREPARATION FOR NEXT MEETING

Assignment. Have the participants read Chapter Nine, "You Can Depend on God's Promises" and review the questions in preparation for next week's session. Encourage them to come to the next session prepared to share their insights on the content of the chapter.

You may also want to assign small groups or particular questions to facilitate next week's meeting time.

F. CLOSING PRAYER

Hold hands, form a circle, and ask for specific prayer requests. Then ask for several volunteers to pray, keeping the prayer requests in mind.

ANSWERS TO BIBLE STUDY APPLICATION

What Does it Mean to Believe?

"To believe" is an act of our will. It is to place confidence in something or someone to the point where you entrust yourself to it. As believers in Christ, we cast ourselves on His finished work on the cross and the written promises of God.

1. Jesus told Thomas to "be not faithless, but believing." Use the verses which follow to answer two basic questions regarding faith.
   a) Describe the relationship between faith and sight. (2 Corinthians 4:18; 5:7; Hebrews 11:1)
   Answers will vary. We don't need faith to believe what we can see. Faith must be exercised in the unseen or spiritual things of life.
   b) Why is our faith is important? (Hebrews 10:39; 11:6)
   Answers will vary. Without faith, we will not be saved and we cannot please God.

2. Match the following statements of faith with the Bible verses that support them.

   a. Religious faith is not based on the wisdom of men, but on the power of God.   **a.** 1 Corinthians 2:5

   b. The object of faith is the Person and work of the Lord Jesus Christ.   **c.** 1 John 5:13

   c. Assurance of salvation is attainable through faith in Jesus Christ.   **d.** James 2:17-26

   d. Living faith leads to good works.   **b.** Acts 4:12 and 1 Corinthians 3:11

We Believe that the Bible is the Inspired Word of God
As Christians, we must know what we believe. Although we cannot see and touch the Lord, we have faith in Him based on the Word of God.

3. The following truths provide a foundation for our belief that the Bible is God's written Word to humankind. Look up the Scriptures below and write them out in the space provided.
   a) 2 Timothy 3:16
      All scripture is given by inspiration of God, and is profitable for doctrine, for reproof, for correction, for instruction in righteousness: that the man of God may be perfect, throughly furnished unto all good works.
   b) 1 Peter 1:20-21
      Knowing this first, that no prophecy of the scripture is of any private interpretation. For the prophecy came not in old time by the will of man: but holy men of God spake as they were moved by the Holy Ghost.

4. Use the following verses to examine how the Word of God was given to the apostles and prophets.
   a) Exodus 20:1
      - According to Moses, who was the author of the Ten Commandments?
        God spoke the words of the Ten Commandments.

   b) 2 Samuel 23:1-3 and Acts 1:16
      - Who spoke "by the mouth of" David?
        The Spirit of the Lord or the Holy Spirit.
      - Whose word was on his tongue?
        God's word was on his tongue.

   c) Jeremiah 36:1-2
      - Who gave the instructions to Jeremiah?
        The word came to Jeremiah from the Lord.
      - Who spoke the words which Jeremiah wrote?
        God spoke to Jeremiah.

   d) Ezekiel 1:3
      - Whose word came to Ezekiel?
        The word of the Lord came to Ezekiel.

- Whose hand was upon him?
  The hand of the Lord was there upon him.

e) Isaiah 6:8-9 and Acts 28:25-26
  - Whose voice spoke to Isaiah and instructed him to go and speak to the people?

  The voice of the Lord.

  - Who spoke to the people "by the mouth of" the prophet Isaiah (or Esaias)?

  The Holy Spirit spoke to the people.

f) Revelation 1:1
  - Who gave the Apostle John the revelation of Jesus Christ?
  God gave John the revelation of Jesus Christ.

We Believe in the Deity of Jesus Christ
Today many regard Jesus as a prophet, a great man, or a good example. However, the foundation of Christianity is the deity of Jesus Christ. The Scriptures declare that Jesus is God, and the heart of every true believer echoes the words of Thomas: "My Lord and my God."

5. Match the following Scripture references with the **divine characteristics** of Jesus Christ.

a. Isaiah 9:6-7; Daniel 7:14; 1 Corinthians 15:27 and Philippians 2:9-11

b. Isaiah 11:2; John 2:24; 16:30 and Colossians 2:3

c. Matthew 18:20; 28:20 and Ephesians 1:23

d. Matthew 28:18 and Ephesians 1:19-21

e. John 8:58; 17:5, 24 and 1 John 1:1

f. Hebrews 13:8 and Revelation 1:17-18

e. Pre-existent—Jesus existed as a distinct person before He came into the world.

a. Pre-eminent—Jesus is above all things except God the Father.

c. Omnipresent—Jesus promises to be present with believers.

d. Omnipotent—Jesus possesses all power in heaven and in earth.

b. Omniscient—Jesus is all-knowing.

f. Eternal—Jesus is alive forevermore.

6. Match the following Scripture references with the **divine offices** of Jesus Christ.

   a. Luke 2:11; John 4:42; 1 John 4:14
   b. John 1:3; Ephesians 3:9; Colossians 1:16; Hebrews 1:2
   c. John 5:28-29; 11:25; 1 Corinthians 15:22
   d. Acts 10:36; Romans 14:9; 1 Corinthians 8:6
   e. Acts 10:42; 2 Timothy 4:1; 2 Corinthians 5:10
   f. Colossians 1:17; Hebrews 1:3
   g. 1 Timothy 2:5; Hebrews 9:15; 12:24

   b. Creator of the Universe
   f. Sustainer of All Things
   g. Mediator between God and Man
   e. Judge of All People
   a. Saviour of the World
   c. Giver of Resurrection Life
   d. Lord of All

7. Read John 5:18-24 to examine some of the **divine claims** of Jesus Christ in His own words. Use the verses in this passage to answer the following questions.

   a) Why were the Jews trying to kill Jesus?
   The Jews understood that Jesus claimed equality with God. Not only was Jesus breaking the laws regarding the Sabbath, but by calling God His own Father, Jesus was making Himself equal with God.

   b) In which of these verses does Jesus claim that:
   - He has the right to receive divine worship and honor.
     Verse 23
   - God is His Father in a unique way.
     Verse 19
   - He has the power to give life and raise the dead.
     Verse 21
   - He maintains unity, communion, and authority with God.
     Verse 20
   - He has the right to judge all people.
     Verse 22
   - He has the power to give eternal life.
     Verse 24

We Believe and Rely on the Finished Work of Jesus Christ
Jesus announced from the cross, "It is finished" (John 19:30). His death

102 *In Step With the Master*

and resurrection provided atonement for our sins and opened a new and living way to God (Hebrews 10:19).

8. Match the following Scripture references with the **divine accomplishments** of Jesus Christ.

a. Ezekiel 36:26-27; John 3:3; 2 Corinthians 5:17
b. Isaiah 53:4-6; 2 Corinthians 5:21
c. Matthew 20:28; 1 Timothy 2:6
d. Matthew 26:28; John 1:29
e. John 14:6; Ephesians 2:18
f. Acts 4:12; Hebrews 7:25
g. Romans 3:26; 4:25; 5:1
h. Romans 5:10; 2 Corinthians 5:18
i. Galatians 3:13-14; 1 Peter 1:18-19
j. Titus 2:14; Hebrews 10:10; 1 Corinthians 6:11
k. 1 John 2:2; 4:10

f. Salvation
c. Ransom for Sin
h. Reconciliation with God
e. Access to God
d. Remission of Sins
g. Justification
j. Sanctification
i. Redemption
a. Regeneration
k. Propitiation
b. Substitution

LIFE APPLICATION

Personal Application

1. What doubts or questions about God are you struggling with right now?

2. Which of the following have you found to be most helpful in times of doubt?
   - The Word of God—the fact that the Bible says it.
   - The Faithfulness of God—evidence of His working on your behalf in the past.
   - Prayer—going honestly before God and saying, "Lord, I believe; help my unbelief."
   - The Faith of Others—seeking out other believers for advice, wisdom, encouragement, and prayer.

3. Note that Jesus answers Thomas' doubts with spiritual evidence. Are you prepared to answer the doubts of others concerning who Jesus is with the Word of God and a personal testimony of His work in your

life? If not, memorize some of the verses from this lesson to become equipped to do so.

4. Do you know what you believe? Using the truths from this Bible Study lesson, write out your personal statement of faith in Jesus Christ. Begin your statement of faith with the words: "I Believe . . . ."

5. The word "atonement" is an all-inclusive word that describes, in general, all that Jesus accomplished for us by His death on the cross. Each day this week:
   - Look up the definition of a doctrinal term from Bible Application question 8 in a dictionary.

   - Select a related verse and meditate on this truth.

   - Thank God in prayer for the atonement for sin made available to us through Jesus Christ the Lord.

Church Ministry Application
1. Does your church have a written Statement of Faith?

2. Are new believers being grounded in truth so that they know what they believe and can communicate their faith in Jesus Christ to others?

3. How are believers who have sincere questions or doubts treated? Is there a time or place (children's ministry, Sunday school, Bible study, etc.) where questions about the Person and work of Jesus Christ or the basic doctrines of Christianity can be answered by truths from the Word of God, as well as the experience of other believers?

SESSION NINE

YOU CAN DEPEND ON GOD'S PROMISES

For sessions of 90 minutes or more, use the lesson format for PART ONE and PART TWO.

PART ONE

ACTIVITY	TIME
Opening Prayer	5 minutes
Scripture Search	10 minutes
Chapter Highlights	20 minutes

PART TWO

ACTIVITY	TIME
Small Group Study	10 minutes
Large Group Presentations	20 minutes
Life Application Discussion	10 minutes
Closing Prayer	5 minutes

For sessions of less than 90 minutes, use PART ONE only and assign the Bible Study Application questions as homework.

Lesson Aims: At the end of this two-part Bible study session, the participants should be able to: a) explain why we can trust God; b) list some of the benefits of trusting God's Word; c) understand that we can trust God at all times.

PART ONE

A. OPENING PRAYER
Open the session with prayer. Include the requests that God would bless each participant to:
- Trust in the Lord with all their hearts.
- Depend and reply upon God's promises in every situation.

B. SCRIPTURE SEARCH
1. As background:
   - Ask someone to read Exodus 3:7-8 aloud to the group.
   - Explain that in the passage of Scripture for this Bible Study lesson, we see that God kept His word. He has delivered the nation of

Israel from bondage and brought them to the land of Canaan, the Promised Land "flowing with milk and honey."

- Before going in to take possession of the land, Moses sends 12 leaders, one from each tribe of Israel, to "spy out" the land.

2. Ask someone to read Numbers 13:17-27 aloud to the group.

3. Ask for volunteers to answer the following questions:
    - What things were the spies told to investigate in the land of Canaan?

    The geography, the fertility, and the fruitfulness of the land; the strength and number of the inhabitants; and the type of cities in which they dwelled.

    - How long did they stay in Canaan?

    They spent 40 days in the land of Canaan.

    - What good report did the 12 leaders agree upon in verse 27?

    They agreed that the land was "flowing with milk and honey" as the Lord had promised.

    - What did they bring back to show the fruitfulness of the land?

    They brought back a cluster of grapes, and some pomegranates and figs.

    - How were the grapes carried?

    They were carried on a staff between two men.

    - What mental picture of the grapes does this description evoke?

    Answers may vary. The cluster of grapes may have been unusually large and heavy.

You Can Depend On God's Promises 107

4. Ask someone to read the negative report from Numbers 13:28-33 aloud to the group.

5. Ask for volunteers to answer the following questions:
    - On what obstacle did the negative report focus?

      The negative report focused on the size and strength of the inhabitants.

    - In contrast, what did Caleb recommend in verse 30?

      Caleb declared, "Let us go up at once, and possess it; for we are well able to overcome it."

    - Whose report did the people believe?
      The people believed the negative report of the 10 spies.

6. Ask someone to read Numbers 14:1-3 aloud to the group.

7. To highlight the significance of these verses:
    - Ask the participants to identify or label the actions of the Israelites in each verse.
      Verse 1: clamoring, whining, crying
      Verse 2: grumbling, murmuring, complaining
      Verse 3: questioning God, predicting the worst, threatening to turn back, thinking that they knew more than God
    - Explain that "trust" is a firm belief in the honesty, truthfulness, justice, or power of a person or thing.

    - Point out that the Israelites' not only demonstrated a lack of trust, they criticized and insulted God. In these three verses, they questioned God's intentions, challenged His honesty, denied His truthfulness, implied that He was unjust, and insinuated that He lacked the power to enable them to prevail against the giants in the land.

8. Ask someone to read Numbers 14:4-11, 27-35 aloud to the group.

9. To conclude the discussion, ask the participants to note that:
    - God is just—In verse 28, the Israelites received punishment

according to the words that they, themselves had spoken.

- God is merciful—In verse 31, although they predicted that their children would perish, God promised to preserve them and bring them into the land of Canaan.

- God is trustworthy—Even in this situation, God kept His promise. Forty years later, He allowed Caleb, Joshua, and the children of the congregation to possess the Promised Land that their parents had despised.

10. Finally, read Joshua 21:43-45 aloud to the class:
"And the Lord gave unto Israel all the land which he sware to give unto their fathers; and they possessed it, and dwelt therein. And the Lord gave them rest round about, according to all that he sware unto their fathers: and there stood not a man of all their enemies before them; the Lord delivered all their enemies into their hand. There failed not ought of any good thing which the Lord had spoken unto the house of Israel; all came to pass."

C. CHAPTER HIGHLIGHTS

Using the content of Chapter Nine background, give a general overview of the chapter. Be sure to include the following topics:
1. God's Promise is Trustworthy
2. Affirming God's Trustworthiness
3. The Effect of a Negative Perception of God's Trustworthiness
4. The Danger of Refusing Divine Faithfulness
5. God is Trustworthy

PART TWO

A. BIBLE STUDY APPLICATION

1. Introduction

The Bible Study Application section contains eight questions which provide an opportunity to examine the importance of trusting God. The discussion of the Bible Study Application questions should confirm that the students understand that in every situation we can trust that God will keep His promises.

Allow as much time as necessary to encourage the exchange of ideas and insights. Use the information preceding each set of questions to help introduce or close the discussion of a topic. Use the Bible verses to help keep the discussion on track. Depending on the size and personality of the group, you can discuss as many or as few of the questions as needed.

   2. Procedure

   Select Small Group Leaders. Ask for volunteers or select five small group leaders. Then assign each small group leader a number from 1-5. (This can also be done beforehand to save time.) Ask the small group leaders to write their numbers on large sheets of white paper so that they can be seen from a distance.

   Divide into Small Groups. Inform the participants that they will be separated into small groups. Each group will study a different set of questions and then will present their findings to the larger group at the end of the study period. The questions should be assigned as follows:

> Group #1: God is True (questions 1-2)
> Group #2: God is Faithful (questions 3-4)
> Group #3: God's Word is Sure (question 5)
> Group #4: The Benefits of Trusting God (question 6)
> Group #5: Whose Report Will You Believe? (questions 7-8)

   Allow Participants to Count Off by Fives. Then ask them to follow the small group leader who is holding their assigned number. Identify the location of each group. (These locations can also be pre-printed on a sheet of paper, photocopied, and distributed to save time.) Participants should then assemble into smaller groups in their respective meeting areas.

   Note: If the Bible Study is small, divide into four groups and eliminate discussion group #4. You may want to include question 6 as part of the homework assignment.

B. SMALL GROUP STUDY

   1. Small Group Leaders

   Each group will have one topic to explore. For each topic, there are questions and related Scripture references to stimulate discussion.

   2. Sharing Insights

   After 15 minutes, designate someone who will summarize the small group discussion within the larger body of participants. Remind the designated person that she or he will only have five minutes to present.

C. LARGE GROUP PRESENTATIONS

   Reconvene the Group. Call the small groups back together.

Explain the Procedure. Explain that a representative of each small group will share that group's reflections on the Bible Study Application questions with the larger group.

Remind Small Group Representatives of the Time. Remind each group representative that he or she should try to summarize the group's discussion in less than five minutes. Allow up to five minutes to discuss each group's presentation.

D. LIFE APPLICATION DISCUSSION*

If time permits, the larger group can then discuss the Personal Application and Church Ministry questions together.

1. Introduction

The Personal Application section contains three questions which encourage the participants to consider the teaching in light of their own lives. The Church Ministry Application section contains three questions which address some implications for the congregation as a whole.

2. Sharing Insights

This discussion should be open-ended and voluntary. The sharing of personal insights or recommendations for church ministry should be encouraged but not required. The group may have quite a bit to say. Watch the clock! Stop them after 10 minutes.

*Answers are not provided for the Personal Application and Church Ministry sections because of the personal or specific nature of the questions.

E. PREPARATION FOR NEXT MEETING

Assignment. Have the participants read Chapter Ten, "You Are Chosen" and review the questions in preparation for next week's session. Encourage them to come to the next session prepared to share their insights on the content of the chapter.

You may also want to assign small groups or particular questions to facilitate next week's meeting time.

F. CLOSING PRAYER

Hold hands, form a circle, and ask for specific prayer requests. Then ask for several volunteers to pray, keeping the prayer requests in mind.

ANSWERS TO BIBLE STUDY APPLICATION

God Is True

1. Fill in the blanks in the verses below to describe God's honesty and truthfulness.
   a) Numbers 23:19
   God is not a man, **that he should lie;** neither the son of man, **that he should repent:** hath he said, and **shall he not do it?** or hath he spoken, and **shall he not make it good?**
   b) Deuteronomy 32:4
   He is the Rock, his work is perfect: for all his ways are judgment: a God of **truth and without iniquity,** just and right is he.
   c) John 3:22
   He that hath received his testimony hath set to his seal that **God is true.**
   d) Titus 1:2
   In hope of eternal life, which God, **that cannot lie,** promised before the world began.

2. Match the following statements concerning Jesus Christ with the verses from the Gospel of John.

   a. Jesus Christ is the truth.
   b. Jesus Christ bears witness to the truth.
   c. Jesus Christ is full of truth.
   d. God's truth is given to us through Jesus Christ.

   c. John 1:14
   d. John 1:17
   a. John 14:6
   b. John 18:37

God Is Faithful

3. Fill in the blanks in the verses below to describe God's faithfulness.
   a) Deuteronomy 7:9
   Know therefore that the Lord thy God, he is God, the faithful God, which **keepeth covenant and mercy with them that love him and keep his commandments to a thousand generations.**
   b) Psalm 33:11
   The counsel of the Lord **standeth for ever,** the thoughts of his heart **to all generations.**

c) Ecclesiastes 3:14
> I know that, whatsoever God doeth, **it shall be forever:** nothing can be put to it, nor any thing taken from it: and God doeth it, that men should fear before him.

d) Malachi 3:6
> For I am the Lord, **I change not;** therefore ye sons of Jacob are not consumed.

e) Romans 11:29
> For the gifts and callings of God are **without repentance.**

f) James 1:17
> Every good and perfect gift is from above, and cometh down from the Father of lights, with whom is **no variableness, neither shadow of turning.**

4. Match the following statements concerning Jesus Christ with the verses in which they are found.

   a. Jesus Christ is the faithful witness.   c. Hebrews 2:17

   b. Jesus Christ is called "Faithful and True."   a. Revelation 1:5

   c. Jesus Christ is our merciful and faithful high priest.   b. Revelation 19:11

God's Word Is Sure

5. Fill in the blanks in the verses below which reveal that God's Word is sure.

   a) Psalm 119:89
   > For ever, O LORD, thy word is **settled in heaven.**

   b) Psalm 119:160
   > Thy word is **true from the beginning:** and every one of thy righteous judgments **endureth for ever.**

   c) Isaiah 40:8
   > The grass withereth, the flower fadeth: but the word of our God **shall stand for ever.**

   d) Isaiah 55:11
   > So shall my word be that goeth forth out of my mouth: **it shall not return unto me void, but it shall accomplish that which I please, and it shall prosper in the thing whereto I sent it.**

   e) Matthew 5:18

For verily I say unto you, Till heaven and earth pass, one jot or one tittle shall in no wise pass from the law, **till all be fulfilled.**

f) Matthew 24:35

Heaven and earth shall pass away, but my words **shall not pass away.**

g) 1 Peter 1:25

But the word of the Lord **endureth for ever.** And this is the word which by the gospel is preached unto you.

The Benefits of Trusting God

6. Match the following Scripture references with the benefits we receive when we trust the Lord.

   a. Jeremiah 17:7 and Psalm 34:8   f. Provision
   b. Nahum 1:7 and Psalm 115:11   b. Protection
   c. Psalm 26:1 and Psalm 125:1   j. Peace
   d. Psalm 32:10 and Hebrews 4:16   h. Direction
   e. Psalm 33:21 and Proverbs 16:20   k. Strength
   f. Psalm 37:3 and Matthew 6:33
   g. Psalm 37:40 and 2 Corinthians 1:10   g. Deliverance
   h. Proverbs 3:5-6 and James 1:5   e. Happiness
   i. Proverbs 18:10 and Proverbs 29:25   i. Safety
   j. Isaiah 26:3 and John 14:27   d. Mercy
   k. Isaiah 26:4 and Philippians 4:13   c. Stability
       a. Blessing

Whose Report Will You Believe?

7. Look up the Scriptures below to identify some of the things in which the Bible tells us *not* to trust.

   a) Jeremiah 17:5 and Psalm 118:8-9

   We should not trust in man.

   b) Jeremiah 17:9 and Proverbs 28:26

   We should not trust our own heart.

   c) Psalm 20:7 and 44:6

   We should not trust in carnal weapons.

   d) Proverbs 11:28 and 1 Timothy 6:17

   We should not trust in riches.

    e) 1 Corinthians 1:9 and 2 Corinthians 3:5
        We should not trust in ourselves.
    f) 1 Corinthians 1:19-20 and 3:19-20
        We should not trust in human wisdom.
    g) 1 Corinthians 1:29; Philippians 3:3; and 1 Peter 1:24-25
        We should not trust in the flesh.

8. Read the following verses from the Book of Psalms to review some of the circumstances in which we can trust God.
    a) Psalm 3:6
        We can trust God even in the face of opposition.
    b) Psalm 23:4
        We can trust God even in the face of death.
    c) Psalm 27:2-3
        We can trust God even when we are attacked by enemies.
    d) Psalm 46:1-2
        We can trust God even in the face of natural disaster.
    e) Psalm 62:8
        We can trust God at all times.

LIFE APPLICATION

Personal Application

1. Seriously consider the following questions:
   - Are there promises in God's Word that you have been afraid that He would not keep?
   - Are there "giant" circumstances in your life that you secretly feel you may be unable to overcome?

2. Now take the following actions:
   - This week begin to write down your fears and list any "giant" or difficult circumstances you may face.

   - At the end of the week, review your list and use a topical bible or concordance to find promises in God's Word which address these concerns or situations.

   - Write the Scripture reference next to each item on the list.

   - During your personal devotions, read these Scriptures over and over until they become God's personal word to you.

- Begin to claim God's promises and thank God in prayer for His Word.

- Then, re-read these verses in context and answer the following questions based on the Scriptures:
    Is there a condition to meet?
    Is there an example to follow?
    Is there a command to obey?
    Is there a sin to avoid?

- Determine that you will trust and obey God in each of these areas. Remember that you can depend on God's promises and allow God to develop your confidence in Him.

3. Finally, review God's faithfulness to you and your family. Encourage others to trust God by sharing your testimony. Remind them that God is "no respecter of persons" (Acts 10:34; Romans 2:11). God always keeps His promises; by His divine nature, He is faithful and true.

Church Ministry Application
1. Our God is trustworthy.
    - How often is the nature of God (including God's faithfulness, truthfulness, justice, and divine power) reviewed or explained from the pulpit?

    - Is the congregation frequently reminded that God "is able to do exceeding abundantly above all that we ask or think, according to the power that worketh in us"?

    - Is the greatness of God praised during the worship service on Sunday morning?

2. God's promises can be trusted even when we are not trustworthy ourselves.
    - Is the truth of 1 John 1:9 communicated in times of personal failure?

    - Is the value of repentance and the promise of forgiveness clearly taught?

3. The promises of God are true for every generation.
    - Are the children in the congregation being prepared to believe and inherit God's promises?
    - Are they being taught the importance of acting in faithful obedience to God's Word?

SESSION TEN

YOU ARE CHOSEN

For sessions of 90 minutes or more, use the lesson format for PART ONE and PART TWO.

PART ONE

ACTIVITY	TIME
Opening Prayer	5 minutes
Scripture Search	10 minutes
Chapter Highlights	20 minutes

PART TWO

ACTIVITY	TIME
Small Group Study	10 minutes
Large Group Presentations	20 minutes
Life Application Discussion	10 minutes
Closing Prayer	5 minutes

For sessions of less than 90 minutes, use PART ONE only and assign the Bible Study Application questions as homework.

Lesson Aims: At the end of this two-part Bible study session, the participants should be able to: a) recognize their value in the sight of God; b) explain the definition of "holiness" and the importance of holy living; c) understand their responsibility as the chosen people of God in the world today.

PART ONE

A. OPENING PRAYER

Open the session with prayer. Include the requests that God would bless each participant to:
- Know that they are special in the sight of God.
- Give praise to God who called them out of darkness into His marvelous light.
- Understand the benefits and responsibilities of being chosen by God.

B. SCRIPTURE SEARCH

1. Ask someone to read Deuteronomy 7:6-11 aloud to the group.

2. Ask for volunteers to answer the following questions:
   - In verse 6, who chose whom?
   God chose the Israelites to be His people.
   - What words are used to describe the people of Israel in God's sight?
   The words "holy" and "special" are used to describe the Israelites in the sight of God (KJV).
   - According to verse 6, why did God choose the Israelites?
   God chose the Israelites to be "a special people unto himself."
   - In your opinion, what does the phrase "unto himself" imply?
   Answers will vary. God desired to reestablish the special relationship between man and God that was broken when Adam sinned. God chose the Israelites above (or over) all the other people on the face of the earth to bring them into relationship with Himself.
   - Verse 7 states that God did not choose Israel because of their great number. Why do you thing this point was made?
   Answers will vary. This statement implies that the Israelites were not chosen by God or considered special in His sight because of some natural attribute, ability, or advantage which they possessed.
   - In verse 8, what two reasons did God give for choosing the Israelites?
   God chose them because He loved them and to keep the oath which He had sworn to their forefathers.
   - According to verse 9, how will God respond to those who love Him and keep His commandments?
   God is faithful to them; He keeps His promises and gives mercy to them and their children forever.
   - According to verse 10, how will God respond to those who hate (or turn against) Him?
   God will repay them openly with inescapable destruction.
   - In verse 11, what are God's people instructed to do?
   God's people are to obey His Word.

C. CHAPTER HIGHLIGHTS

Using the content of Chapter Ten background, give a general overview of the chapter. Be sure to include the following topics:
1. You Are Chosen by God
2. Why Did God Choose You?
3. The Benefits of Being Chosen by God
4. Chosen for Responsibility

PART TWO

A. BIBLE STUDY APPLICATION

1. Introduction

The Bible Study Application section contains six questions which provide an opportunity to examine the privilege of being chosen by God. The discussion of the Bible Study Application questions should confirm that the students understand the responsibilities of God's chosen people.

Allow as much time as necessary to encourage the exchange of ideas and insights. Use the information preceding each set of questions to help introduce or close the discussion of a topic. Use the Bible verses to help keep the discussion on track. Depending on the size and personality of the group, you can discuss as many or as few of the questions as needed.

2. Procedure

Select Small Group Leaders. Ask for volunteers or select four small group leaders. Then assign each small group leader a number from 1-4. (This can also be done beforehand to save time.) Ask the small group leaders to write their numbers on large sheets of white paper so that they can be seen from a distance.

Divide into Small Groups. Inform the participants that they will be separated into small groups. Each group will study a different set of questions and then will present their findings to the larger group at the end of the study period. The questions should be assigned as follows:

Group #1: A Chosen Generation (questions 1-2)
Group #2: A Royal Priesthood (questions 3-4)
Group #3: A Holy Nation (question 5)
Group #4: A Peculiar People (question 6)

Allow Participants to Count Off by Fours. Then ask them to follow the small group leader who is holding their assigned number. Identify the location of each group. (These locations can also be pre-printed on a sheet of paper, photocopied, and distributed to save time.) Participants should then assemble into smaller groups in their respective meeting areas.

B. SMALL GROUP STUDY

1. Small Group Leaders

Each group will have one topic to explore. For each topic, there are questions and related Scripture references to stimulate discussion.

2. Sharing Insights

After 10 minutes, designate someone who will summarize the small group discussion within the larger body of participants. Remind the designated person that she or he will only have five minutes to present.

C. LARGE GROUP PRESENTATIONS

Reconvene the Group. Call the small groups back together.

Explain the Procedure. Explain that a representative of each small group will share that group's reflections on the Bible Study Application questions with the larger group.

Remind Small Group Representatives of the Time. Remind each group representative that he or she should try to summarize the group's discussion in less than five minutes. Allow up to five minutes to discuss each group's presentation.

D. LIFE APPLICATION DISCUSSION*

If time permits, the larger group can then discuss the Personal Application and Church Ministry questions together.

1. Introduction

The Personal Application section contains three questions which encourage the participants to consider the teaching in light of their own lives. The Church Ministry Application section contains three questions which address some implications for the congregation as a whole.

2. Sharing Insights

This discussion should be open-ended and voluntary. The sharing of personal insights or recommendations for church ministry should be encouraged but not required. The group may have quite a bit to say. Watch the clock! Stop them after 10 minutes.

*Answers are not provided for the Personal Application and Church Ministry sections because of the personal or specific nature of the questions.

F. CLOSING PRAYER

Hold hands, form a circle, and ask for specific prayer requests. Then ask for several volunteers to pray, keeping the prayer requests in mind.

ANSWERS TO BIBLE STUDY APPLICATION

A Chosen Generation

In the Old Testament, God chose the Israelites to be His people (Deuteronomy 7:6). Under God's new covenant established through the blood of Jesus Christ, we have been chosen to be God's people as members of the Church—the body of Christ.

1. In Deuteronomy 7:8, God tells the people of Israel that it was because He loved them and kept the oath He made to their forefathers that He has set His affection upon them.

    - Because of whom has God set His affection on us as believers? (Ephesians 1:6)

    - His Son Jesus Christ.

    - Why did Christ die for us? (Titus 2:14)

    - Christ died that He might redeem us from all iniquity, and purify unto Himself a peculiar people, zealous of good works.

    - Why did God choose to save us? (Titus 3:5-6)

    - God chose to save us, not because of our own righteousness or good works, but because of His mercy.

    - Instead of the Promised Land, what will we inherit? (Titus 3:7) We will inherit eternal life.

2. Look up the following verses and use them to answer the questions below.
    a) John 15:5, 16
        - In verse 16, who chose whom?
          Our Lord Jesus Christ chose us to be His people.
        - For what purpose have we been chosen?
          That we should go and bring forth fruit and that our fruit would remain.
        - How do we become spiritually fruitful?
          We must abide or remain in Christ and allow Him to abide in us.
        - Is there any other way to live a fruitful Christian life?
          No, apart from Christ we can do nothing.
    b) Ephesians 1:4
        - When did God choose us?
          God chose us before the foundation of the world.
        - How were we chosen?
          We were chosen in Christ to become the people of God.
        - As God's chosen people, how should we conduct ourselves in this world?
          We should be holy and without blame before God in love.
    c) 1 Peter 2:9
        - What four phrases are used to describe God's people?
          The four phrases used are: a chosen generation, a royal priesthood, an holy nation, and a peculiar people.
        - For what purpose have we been chosen?
          To show forth the praises of God who has called us out of darkness into His marvelous light.

A Royal Priesthood
In the Old Testament, the priests would offer sacrifices to God on behalf of the people and communicate directly with God. Now through Jesus Christ, every Christian has been made a priest before God.

3. Match the statements below with the verses that support them. (A statement may be associated with more than one Scripture reference.)

a. All believers have direct access to God through Jesus Christ.
b. All believers are commanded to live holy lives.
c. All believers are to offer up "spiritual sacrifices" unto God.
d. All believers must intercede and pray for others.

c. Romans 12:1-2
d. 1 Timothy 2:1-4
b. 1 Peter 1:14-16
c. 1 Peter 2:5
a. Hebrews 4:16 and 10:19
c. Hebrews 13:15-16

4. Fill in the blanks in the following verses from the Book of Revelation which describe the present and future priesthood of those who believe in Christ.
    - Revelation 1:5-6
        And from Jesus Christ, who is the faithful witness, and the first begotten of the dead, and the prince of the kings of the earth. Unto him that loved us, and washed us from our sins in his own blood, And hath made us **kings and priests unto God and his Father;** to him be glory and dominion for ever and ever. Amen.
    - Revelation 20:6
        Blessed and holy is he that hath part in the first r esurrection: on such the second death hath no power, but they shall be **priests of God and of Christ, and shall reign with him a thousand years.**

A Holy Nation
Holiness describes both the nature of God and the way of life intended for His people. The word "holy" means separate from sin, pure, sacred, clean; set apart to God for His glory. We serve a holy God. What is true of the Father must also become true of His children.

5. Read the following verses and use them to answer the questions below.
    a) Romans 6:22
        - What kind of fruit should our lives produce?

        - As God's chosen people, our lives should produce the fruit of holiness.

        - What will we receive as a result?

        - We will receive everlasting life.

b) 2 Corinthians 6:16—7:1
- In verse 16, what phrase is used to describe the people of God?
  The people of God are called "the temple of the living God."
- What does this description mean?
  It means that God Himself will dwell in us and walk in us; and He will be our God and we will be His people.
- When we separate ourselves from sin and unrighteousness, what will happen?
  God says that He will receive us, and He will be a Father to us and we will be His children.
- In light of these promises, what should we do?
  We should cleanse ourselves from all filthiness of the flesh and spirit, perfecting holiness in the fear of God.

c) Hebrews 12:14
- Why should we be holy?
  Without holiness, no one will see the Lord.

d) 1 Peter 1:15
- Why should we be holy?
  We should be holy because God is holy.

e) Revelation 22:11-12
- Why should we be holy?
  The Lord Jesus Christ will return in judgment and give reward or repayment to every person according to their work.

A Peculiar People

We are not our own. We are God's people, His treasured possession. We did not choose God; He chose us and redeemed us, at a great price. We belong to the Lord, and we are special in His sight.

6. Fill in the blanks in the following verses describe God's people.
   a) Exodus 19:5
       Now therefore, if ye will obey my voice indeed, and keep

my covenant, then ye shall be **a peculiar treasure unto me above all people:** for all the earth is mine:

b) Deuteronomy 14:2

For thou art an holy people unto the Lord thy God, and the Lord hath chosen thee to be **a peculiar people unto himself, above all the nations that are upon the earth.**

c) 1 Samuel 12:22

For the Lord will not forsake his people for his great name's sake: because **it hath pleased the Lord to make you his people.**

d) Psalms 100:3

Know ye that the Lord he is God: it is he that hath made us, and not we ourselves; **we are his people, and the sheep of his pasture.**

e) John 10:27-28

My sheep hear my voice, and I know them, and they follow me: And I give unto them **eternal life; and they shall never perish, neither shall any man pluck them out of my hand.**

f) 1 Corinthians 6:19-20

What? know ye not that **your body is the temple of the Holy Ghost which is in you,** which ye have of God, and **ye are not your own?** For ye are bought with a price: therefore glorify God in your body, and in your spirit, which are God's.

g) Hebrews 8:10

For this is the covenant that I will make with the house of Israel after those days, saith the Lord; I will put my laws **into their mind, and write them in their hearts:** and I will be to them **a God, and they shall be to me a people.**

LIFE APPLICATION

Personal Application

1. How does it make you feel to know that you are:

- Chosen—Selected by God to be the object of His love and mercy?
- Royalty—Related to the King of kings?
- God's Possession—Set apart for God's use, by God's high and holy calling?
- A Member of the Priesthood of Believers—Representing God to humanity?

2. Evaluate your prayer life. How much time are you spending with the King?

3. We walk in holiness by becoming like Christ, being dedicated to God, and living to please Him. How separate are you from the world and its ways? How does God's call to holiness challenge you:
   - At work?
   - At home?
   - In the community?
   - In the church

Church Ministry Application
1. Is the joy, wonder, and awe of being God's chosen and treasured possession revealed in the worship service, preached from the pulpit, and experienced by the members of the congregation?

2. How faithfully are you and the members of your congregation practicing the priesthood before God and others?

3. We are called to be witnesses (Acts 1:8). How faithfully are you and other members declaring God's praises to a dark world?